Life Filled with God's Best

JODY CHADBAN

PRODIGAL PRESS

Copyright © 2015 Jody Chadban
All rights reserved.
No part of this book may be reproduced in any written, electronic, recording, or photocopying form without written permission of the author, Jody Chadban.

ISBN-13: 978-0-9897020-3-4

Table of Contents

Chapter 1: The Handbag 1

Chapter 2: Show Me the Money 27

Chapter 3: I Never Did Care for Fancy Packaging 47

Chapter 4: You Can Tell it's a Fake 67

Chapter 5: The Land of the Boutique 87

Chapter 6: It's a Standout 107

Chapter 7: This Season's Must-haves 127

Chapter 8: Take it out of the
           Display Case and Let's Get Started 149

Dedication

To the man of my dreams, the one my soul loves, my husband and best friend: Thank you for your love, belief, encouragement, wisdom, and extravagance that you pour over me every day of my life. Thank you for leading us in this adventurous, faith-filled life to the full. I'm forever grateful for our yesterdays, and so excited about our tomorrows.

To my exquisite children, Madeline and Gabriel: I love you both with every part of my being. You are the sunshine of my life, and fill my heart to overflowing. Thank you for embracing the life we lead with such courage and joy. You continually amaze me. I pray that you would forever live a life that defies the ordinary and changes the world.

1

THE HANDBAG

"Then the Lord took Abram outside and said to him, "Look up into the sky and count the stars if you can. That's how many descendants you will have!" And Abram believed the Lord, and the Lord counted him as righteous because of his faith." Genesis 15:4-6 (NLT)

Has anyone ever told you to stop and smell the roses? It's a concept we are all familiar with and have varying degrees of success in. It's an ideal I am getting a lot better with. I am learning more and more how to not rush through life so fast the scenery becomes a blur. Because when we really do stop and take in all that is happening around us, we're able to see the most profound life lessons in the most normal of circumstances.

It was in one such period of my life when God poured a message into my spirit that appeared so basic and yet unraveled a depth and complexity that still takes my breath away. The lessons He revealed to me through handbags I carried with me every day, have enabled me to step into the dreams I didn't even know existed in my heart.

We know from Cinderella that a pair of shoes has the power to change your life, but I never imagined that a Prada handbag could change the course of mine.

CONCRETE JUNGLE WHERE DREAMS ARE MADE

A handbag is an important part of a woman's life. There is an emotional attachment to handbags that makes little sense to the males in our world. I have an entire board on my Pinterest account dedicated to handbags that I love. You may not be at that level of interest, but to some degree there is something wired into our DNA as women that appreciates a nice looking bag.

The bag you are carrying over your arm or shoulder is so much more than a mode of transport for your personal belongings. There are many layers to these carriers. Your handbag is one of the first things women look at when seeing you for the first time. For New Yorkers especially, the handbag you carry and the name on that bag, weighs heavily in the 15-20 seconds of observation and subsequent judgment call that is made of you. Fairly or unfairly, the right handbag can open doors just as quickly as the wrong one can close them. And as ridiculous or absurd as this might seem, this is just how it is. It doesn't matter if we like it or not, that's New York!

New York City is a place like no other. It is a city of glamour and magnificence, as well as loneliness and heartbreak. The intensity of this city leaves you breathless. This place will either make your spirit soar, or crush it completely. The first is true for me. I love this city. I love the people of this city. I love the women of this city.

This city inspires me to dream big, live big, love big, and fight the good fight like no other place I know.

One of my favorite things to do in New York is to walk the city streets. There is something about these streets that puts an extra spring in your step. On every street and avenue you see all sorts of women and the handbags they carry with them throughout their day. At any given time you'll be able to spot everything from Prada to Guess, from Chanel to Target, you may even spot a plastic bag, or a trolley. Everywhere you look, as far as the eye can see, you will see women with their chosen handbag.

The range of handbags available in New York City is as diverse as the women who carry them. There seems to be no end to the variety and abundance of handbags. Store after store stocks handbags in all shapes, colors, textures, sizes, and price ranges. The possibilities are endless. Who could have imagined that something as basic as a purse would become such a staple for women everywhere?

Age is no barrier for the love of handbags. From little girls to elderly women, the love of handbags surpasses all demographics. A classic Louis Vuitton looks at home on the arm of a 20-something in Brooklyn, just as it would on an 84-year-old Grandmother on the Upper East Side.

New York women are not the only ones who have such a strong attachment to handbags. Culture is no barrier for this love. From London to Paris to Sydney to Capetown, women all over the world share the joy and love of handbags. Handbags are a universal language for women. A good handbag holds currency no matter where in the world you venture. It is almost like handbags have the power to break down cultural differences.

THAT WHICH BONDS US TOGETHER

When I first started work in New York, I met a beautiful older woman who was in leadership over me. I wanted to connect with her and develop a strong relationship, but I worried about how I would achieve this. What could I say? How could I engage her? To my absolute surprise, she walked up to me and said, "Nice Louis!" I muttered, "Thank you". As she walked away, I looked down incredulously at my Louis Vuitton hanging off my arm and smiled at the interaction that had just taken place. No matter how different our worlds were, how different we appeared to be, there was this common thread that connected us. It wasn't the fact that we both love Jesus; it was the truth that we both love Louis Vuitton!

On a different occasion, I was flying from LAX to JFK. After surviving the initial leg of my journey (from Sydney to LAX, which is always the worst part), I was keen to sit and have a chat. My daughter, Madeline, had fallen asleep before we had even taken off and so I looked to the young lady on the other side of me wondering if she was up for a conversation. The lady seemed reluctant in the beginning to get too involved in conversation. That was until the subject turned to handbags. She instantly came to life and made herself very comfortable in the seat beside me. She started to talk about the great adventure she was on, literally crossing from one side of the US to the other in pursuit of *the* bag. She had done her research and knew her stuff and was confident that she would know it when she saw it. I was fascinated by this woman's commitment to finding and purchasing the perfect handbag.

Although they are closely linked to our identity as women, it would be a mistake to think a women's handbag is exclusively hers.

THE HANDBAG

Any mother, wife, or girlfriend will agree with me that the men and children in our lives are continually handing us items to keep safe in our bags. If you stopped women on the street and peeked inside her handbag, I guarantee there would be more items in there that did not belong to her than those that did.

If my handbag is feeling particularly heavy, I'll reach in and find superhero figurines, Stuart's (my husband) sunglasses, my daughter's phone, multiple wallets, lip balm, and the list goes on. Then there are all the items I have added for my family that they don't even think of, but I figure they may need. I think ahead and make sure there are enough tissues for the whole family, Band-Aids, sanitizer (for when my children inevitably have to use a public restroom), colored pencils, and a myriad of other things.

Handbags always start off with plenty of room, lots of secret, empty compartments, but all too soon the bag is filled to the brim and is as heavy as lead. No matter how big the bag, you will inevitably fill to the size that you have. It's like the goldfish rule. A goldfish will grow to the size of the tank that it is housed in. The bigger the tank, the bigger the goldfish will grow. The bigger the bag, the more contents you will put inside it.

We were sitting at a cafe one day in Australia, having some lunch as a family. I had placed my handbag on the ground in between Stuart and I. Something was spilled at the table, and I quickly reached for my handbag to get extra tissues. In my haste, I knocked my handbag over. To my horror, a huge piece of crumbed chicken (aka "snitty") fell out of my bag and onto the floor. My family looked at me in disbelief. *What on earth?* I had wrapped up the chicken at the meal the night before thinking my son might eat it later. I had clearly forgotten to take it out of my bag. It was then I knew things had gotten a little out of control.

THE MARY POPPINS FACTOR

No matter what it may be carrying, there is a certain mystery that surrounds a woman's handbag. Growing up there was always an unspoken rule that you didn't go through my mum's handbag. It was a total no-go zone. If you wanted something out of there that was yours, you would take the handbag to Mum, not get it out yourself. Even when my Dad wanted something out of Mum's handbag, he would take the entire bag to her and she would hand over exactly what he needed. I can still hear my Dad's words, "You never go through a woman's handbag."

What is it about a woman's handbag that holds such a mystery?

It has been the very beauty and mystery of a handbag, which has unlocked truths behind even greater mysteries for me. God started to use handbags as a physical representation, a metaphor, to teach and guide me in His ways and heart. Instead of just seeing a handbag as an accessory that I carried with me through my days, I started to see my handbag as representing a vessel for the things I carry as a woman through life.

The more I opened myself to God's words the more depth I started to see in this analogy. I saw a woman's handbag as symbolic of the hopes, dreams, visions, which frame their world. A handbag houses and stores and carries these hopes and dreams. There is a profound unity of spirit for all women in this, as well as providing for a breadth and diversity that is nothing short of magnificent.

Just as other women look and value the type of handbag you

carry, they are also observing and assessing the dreams, hopes, purposes and destinies attached to you. In a place like New York, where the handbag you carry can determine the doors or connections open to you, so too can the dreams you are believing for and holding onto, open pathways and doors and networks. How do other people see what you are carrying? What does the appearance of your handbag look like to the world?

Part of the richness and beauty of this metaphor is the scope and range and type of handbags that exist. This message isn't contained or limited to one style of handbag or woman, but rather works with each and every one. Just as every woman is free to choose the handbag that resounds within her, so too are we free to choose the hopes and dreams that resound within us to frame our world. Everyone appears different, and yet is bound together with a united thread. The mandate is the same for all, but the way it is expressed is uniquely beautiful. We are all women, same in form and function and value, and yet the diversity and flavors and assortment of women and the dreams within them, is amazing.

Just as the handbags we carry are not exclusively for our own personal use, so too the dreams and hopes we carry go far beyond ourselves. As women, what we take hold of and carry the weight and responsibility for, provides for those around us. Dreams are for the whole family! When we carry the dreams and hopes and purposes for our family, we are carrying inheritance and legacy and influence. And at times this can feel heavy. At times this makes our arms ache. There will be seasons where it hurts and stretches us to keep carrying those dreams that we hold for others. But we carry them because we can. We carry them because we have what they don't. My eight-year-old son Gabriel does not carry a handbag. I do! So I will carry what he needs to bring, because I can do that for him. We have as women, the capacity to carry for others.

We need to be mindful of what we are carrying. When all of a sudden the handbag feels so heavy, we stop and look in and see exactly what we have in there. There is a natural purging that takes place as we try and empty our bags of unnecessary items. There will be times when we need to look closely at exactly what we are carrying through life that is attached to our hopes and dreams. When days come that suddenly feel heavy, we need to stop and look and do a purging of anything in our lives that is not necessary for us to carry; for ourselves or anyone else.

There is truth in the principle which says the bigger the bag the more you will fit it. This also applies to our dreams and hopes and destinies. The bigger the landscape, the more room we leave open for God to work in our lives, the more our lives will be filled. How important that we are mindful as to what we are allowing into those spaces in our lives. May we be overflowing with the presence of God and all the fruit that comes from being filled by His Spirit.

What an awesome thing, to see the beautiful rhythm of two mysteries working together. The handbag, and a God in Heaven who knows you by name and created you and knew you while you were still in your mother's womb. Yet our God is so great that human minds can hardly comprehend His true majesty. It is the very essence of this mystery that we carry with us as women, and we take into our days as a vessel to carry all that God has for us.

Women carry the mother heart of God. There is a certain awe, wonder and mystery about this. It is something that we treasure and value and see as holy. There is a sense of not wanting to intrude on what a woman has cultivated and prepared and is carrying on behalf of the ones she loves. As part of this role, women provide a safe environment for those they love by storing the things that are precious or necessary for living well. Some of what a mother carries has been entrusted to her to care for and protect. Yet there is more that the mother carries which is born out of her own foresight and intuition.

A mother's heart loves, protects, perseveres, fights, enables, cares and provides. A mother's heart carries the weight of what those around her need to fulfill the plans and purposes God has for them. She keeps everything together, providing a unity of cause, purpose and provision. She holds the wellspring in her hands and those in her family come and take from it.

What an awesome privilege and responsibility it is to hold such a role, to be trusted and equipped with so much. What an honor to carry the handbag of Heaven! The handbag of Heaven… it sounds so amazing! What does it look like?

THE HANDBAG OF HEAVEN

We all know there are handbags, and then there are *handbags*. You know what I mean? There are the everyday, nice, usual handbags, and then there are the top-shelf, high-end designer bags. The second group are the bags dreams are made of. Mostly unattainable to the average woman, designer bags are works of art in their own right. Brands such as Prada, Louis Vuitton, Chanel are the crème da la crème of the handbag industry. These beauties are what all others are modeled from. They are featured on runways, glossy magazines, and are the "it" accessory for every supermodel, actress, celebrity, and anyone else with influence.

If you are carrying one of these bags on your arm, you are carrying quite an investment. A significant purchase has been made to attain one of these bags, and you are a serious player. These bags aren't for the faint hearted, and owning one is a delight reserved for those fortunate enough to have the funds required to make one yours.

When you have a designer handbag, you are very careful about what is put inside. You are not going to let just any old thing be tossed into your Prada handbag. No half-sucked candy, leaky pens, smeared lip-gloss or used tissues in this handbag. This is a place of beauty and excellence.

So how much does this type of bag cost?

THE PRICE WE PAY

There is an unspoken rule when it comes to shopping for the designer handbag. When entering into this market, there are certain parameters in place. The first thing you notice, as soon as you start shopping in this arena, is that the prices are very hard to find. As you scan the shelves there are no price signs displayed, no bins labeled "Nothing over $1500," no tags hanging from the handles of the bag that you can tilt your head and try to read. If you want to know the price, you are going to have to ask the sales assistant. They will then take the bag of your interest and place it on the counter in front of you. Then they go directly to a concealed zippered section and pull out a small envelope. It is this envelope that holds the price. As the sales assistant opens the envelope, it feels like you are watching the Oscars. *And the Oscar goes to… And the price of this bag is...* And like the sting of hearing a name that isn't yours, you hear a price that is completely beyond your reach. Just as the actors and actresses continue to smile as they nod in "excitement" for the winner, you continue to smile as you nod in thanks and mumble something about going away to think about it. There is nothing to think about. The sales assistant knows this as well as you do. The moment you asked the price, the sales assistant knew the outcome. You see, the unspoken rule in this environment is that if you have to ask how much a bag costs, you probably can't afford it.

There is no question about whether these bags are worth the price. They are exquisite, and just by looking at one you can see the level of workmanship and attention to detail. From the meticulous stitched seams, to the shiny padlocks, to the silk lining, these bags are worth every cent of their asking price. You do not pick up a Prada and think, "What a rip off!"

For the true designer handbag shopper, price will not determine what bag will be purchased. For the women in this market, price is not the deciding factor. If you are seriously shopping for a designer handbag, when you see the one that makes your heart leap, you decide right then and there, "that is the one!" Some of you may be nodding as you remember finding your designer handbags in the past—reminiscing about how you knew it was the one as soon as you saw it. Others of you may identify more with the moment of being told a bag you liked was $2000 and trying to keep it together and not run out of that place as fast as you could in embarrassment. Or still others of you are completely blown away by all of this. Wherever you stand, the rule remains for us all. If you have to ask how much it costs, you can't afford it.

It is because of the exclusive price tag these highly sought after bags are held in such high esteem. Some will do everything they can to save enough money to purchase one of these bags. Some will dip into their funds, making these purchases a priority and reality. Others may use resources handed down to them from past generations. And others will count themselves out completely and not even think about or imagine themselves with such a bag. Where do you fit in?

Remember how I told you that God poured a message into my spirit? Well it's through these designer handbags (definitely not ordinary) that God began to teach me about His plans for our lives. These designer handbags can be likened to the dreams, plans, purposes, destinies, and callings that God has in store for each one of us. They are exclusive, designer-made, hand-crafted, and a work of art. There is nothing ordinary or average about His purposes or calling for our lives. They are top-shelf, crème da la crème, the very best there is. And they are available to every single one of us. But are we in the market? Can we come into His presence and when we see what He has for us, say, "Yes, thank you! I'll take it!!" Or do we have to ask the question? Do we have to first find out how much it is going to cost? And then once we find out, do we fake smile our way back out of His presence and leave empty handed?

As soon as we ask how much it is going to cost, we admit we haven't got what it takes.

What does it take? What does it take to walk down Fifth Avenue and enter Prada, look around the boutique, and when you see a bag that makes your heart leap, instantly say, "I'll take it!" What do we have to possess to be in that position? You need to have a level of resource that will more than cover the cost of the handbag. You have a rough idea of how much these bags cost, and you are confident that wherever on that spectrum this bag lies, you have got it well and truly taken care of. In fact, you have such a level of resource that buying this bag will not leave you lacking in any other area of your life. This will be an investment that will bring you joy and fulfillment and something of worth. If you only have a certain amount of money in your account, it is too risky to say, "I'll have it", without first checking to see if what you have will cover it. You may be fine, able to spend up and make the purchase. There's also a chance that you could come up short, and make even the basics (like putting food on the table), something of a nightmare. No one wants to make an investment of this magnitude and leave the rest of your life skinned.

What does it take to see what God has for us, to feel our heart leap at the thought, and then say, "Yes God, I'll take it!"? What does it take to not even stop to ask, "What is this going to cost?" Like the handbag, there has to be such a level of resource within us that we are confident enough to go for it and take the dream, without leaving the rest of our lives in lack. Gutsy or stupid? The difference is determined by how much treasure we have in our lives. We are constantly given opportunities in life to store up our treasure in Heaven. Day after day, we choose where we want our treasure to lie. Those day-to-day choices impact on our ability to take the big-ticket items. If we lead a life that puts value and resource in the things of this world, those things that we can see, feel, touch, make sense of, be able to control, we will be lacking in Kingdom resource. We will not have enough to shop with the big guns. We will come up short.

Resource in this context is built by leading a life that is governed by the principles of Heaven. The total sacrifice of laying down our lives unlocks an inheritance and heavenly treasure that we can pick up as resource. Our salvation is free. We need nothing when we kneel at the feet of Jesus and ask him to forgive our sins and save us for eternity. But once we have this gift of salvation, we choose daily to take God at His word, to put our own selfish motives down, and to live a life that brings glory to God and identifies us as His heir. We build Kingdom resource when we are about our Father's business and love God more than anything else in this world.

PUBLIC VS. PRIVATE

There is a line of thought that says you can't be any greater in public than you are in private. This means if you aren't doing the hard work in private, you won't be able to produce the goods in the public arena. Athletes get this. How many times do you hear Olympic athletes talk about their training regime after they have been successful and won a medal? The public victory makes all of the hours and years of hard solitary training worth it. How much greater is the prize when we look at this spiritually? 1 Corinthians 9:24-27 "Don't you realize that in a race everyone runs, but only one person gets the prize? So run to win! All athletes are disciplined in their training. They do it to win a prize that will fade away, but we do it for an eternal prize. So I run with purpose in every step. I am not just shadowboxing. I discipline my body like an athlete, training it to do what it should."

If we want to have the level of resource we need to be able to see what God is offering us and take it without hesitation, we need to train and apply ourselves with purpose in every step. What does this kind of training look like? This training requires us to push down our flesh and strengthen our inner man, strengthen our spirit. When you pray, when you fast, when you give, you deny your flesh and build your spirit. This training will result in us being spiritually fit and able to run in a way that we will win. When we become strong and spiritually fit, we will care less about what the world thinks and hold to what God thinks. When I first started to train hard and go after the Prada in my life, one of the initial strengths I learned was to value the applause of Heaven above everything else. If I didn't receive earthly praise or accolades for what I knew God was asking me to do, I trained myself spiritually to not let it hinder my progress. As I continued to train, and be in the word every day, and fast whenever He called me to, and give until it made me scared, and fall to my knees and pray in the spirit, I became stronger. There came this strength within me that wasn't affected, wasn't tossed and turned by the opinions of others. I started to not doubt myself or need constant affirmation from others. I could step down from any platform or situation, and the applause of Heaven that rang in my ears was all I needed to hear. Of course, I would always appreciate and value encouragement from others, but I wasn't reliant on it to buoy my spirits. This set not only strength, but also a resolve within me to go after more.

    Nothing God does is out of sequence or timing. I can look back now and see how necessary it was for God to train me in this area before any other. The truth is, in order to not only see what God has for you, but to be strong enough to aim for it, you have to be operating in the spiritual and not relying on what the world may or may not give to you. Our earthly bodies are just too weak and could never handle it. We can never do enough in our own strength to qualify us for the God dreams. We just haven't got what it takes in ourselves alone. It is only when we come into a partnership with God, and let Jesus be our way, truth, and life, that we have what we need from Him in order to be more than enough. God will only let you see what it is He wants to give you when you are operating in the spiritual, because what He has for you will never work in the natural. In fact, we are blind to it in the natural. Therefore, the promise stands. If He lets you see it, it is yours for the taking! You just need to come prepared to shop.

THE NATURAL VS. THE SPIRITUAL

In the very beginning of the Bible in Genesis, we read that God created the heavens and the earth. These are two very distinct environments and spheres of existence. We live here on earth, which can also be known as the natural. The natural is simply the reality we can see, smell, touch, hear, and make sense of. The natural is an environment where we are encouraged to be in control. We spend our lives managing our world, creating the outcomes we want to see realized, striving for the goals we have set, and doing whatever we can to have the best life we could ever hope to achieve. There are hurts and disappointments in the natural. We are taught that "life wasn't meant to be easy," to "roll with the punches," and that "you can't keep a good man (woman) down". There are a myriad of expressions all meaning that life isn't fair so just deal with it and get on with it as best as you can. Life is whatever you decide to make it, and it's up to you to play the cards destiny has dealt.

To live solely in the natural is, of course, to ignore the spiritual or the supernatural. Yes, God made the earth and everything in it, and He created us to rule over this space. But God also created the heavens. And it is in this heavenly sphere where the spiritual life exists. This is the space where God rules, operating under His principles, and where the Kingdom of light and the kingdom of darkness reside. This is where battles rage every moment of every day between good and evil. This is the home of God and His angels, and where the devil and his demons are at work. The natural was never meant to be lived in without the understanding of the spiritual. There is another whole layer of existence that is operating above us, that we can go through life and never actually acknowledge. We are spiritual beings. We have been created with a body to live in the natural but we also have a spirit that hungers for the spiritual. People look to fill this spiritual emptiness in many different ways. We were made for more than what this world can offer us in the natural. When we live with a spiritual framework in our lives, we carry an authority that isn't possible in the natural.

The truth is we will never really be satisfied in life unless we allow ourselves to look beyond the natural and connect to the supernatural. We will never truly understand life to the full until we allow our spirits to operate on a higher level than what we can see.

Although the natural and the spiritual are intrinsically linked, co-exist, and can be seen like two different layers of the same delicious cake, they are also very different. In fact, it can often feel like one is the exact opposite of the other. Unlike the natural where seeing is believing, the spiritual is all about not seeing but still believing. The natural unfolds in the world around us for all to see, and yet the spiritual happens on a deeply personal level, in the intimate places of our hearts and minds.

We read in Matthew 16 Jesus challenging the religious leaders of the time about this very thing. It says in verses 2 and 3, "He replied, "You know the saying, 'Red sky at night means fair weather tomorrow; red sky in the morning means foul weather all day.' You know how to interpret the weather signs in the sky, but you don't know how to interpret the signs of the times!'" Jesus is saying these leaders are very good at operating in the natural, seeing what is happening here on earth and being able to read it. But they have no understanding of what is happening in the supernatural or the spiritual. Here was Jesus, the Son of God, who had performed many miracles before them, yet they were still demanding miracles to come out of the sky. They wanted to see God work within the frameworks of what they could understand. These leaders had no understanding of the spiritual and could only operate from a natural mindset.

So often we live our lives with a natural one-dimensional mindset. We believe what we see and take life at face value. On the surface it appears to be much easier to navigate life simply with a natural filter rather than entertaining any deeper contexts. It is a trap that all sorts of people have fallen into since the beginning of time.

The natural is a reflection of the spiritual. We see the effects in the natural of what has taken place in the unseen spiritual. The spiritual or supernatural is the highest way to live. We will never have more power, authority, influence, provision, blessing, or favor as when we align ourselves with the principles of Heaven and operate with a spiritual mindset. Yes, the spiritual is far beyond the natural.

Isaiah 55:8-9, "My thoughts are nothing like thoughts," says the Lord. "And my ways are far beyond anything you could imagine. For just as the heavens are higher than the earth, so my ways are higher than your ways and my thoughts higher than your thoughts."

Jesus taught that we must give up our life in order to truly have life. And so we see the very heart of these opposite yet parallel worlds. To have everything we dream about having in the natural, we must do the opposite of what seems logical in the natural in the spiritual. You want to be a powerful leader? You must become a humble servant. You want to wield a level of influence over others? You must consider others to be greater than yourself. You want to be blessed financially? You must give of your very best back to God first.

The spiritual is the land of the great unknown wrapped in the mystery of God. It doesn't make sense. There is no natural logic involved. There are no reasonable explanations. It is grand and captivating and puzzling; it's the space where outcomes we could never have dreamed of are achieved. It is a greenhouse for the above and beyond.

Because the Prada life doesn't make sense in the natural, you have to be really strong in the spiritual before you can even contemplate taking it on. It is impossible to please God without faith. Every step of this journey will be based in faith leading right up to the point where you commit without even having to check the cost. That's faith in its truest form, "the absolute assurance of things hoped for…"

God wants you to see and taste, in the spiritual, what He has planned. When it is birthed in the spiritual, it will continue in the spiritual. There is no room for worldly mindsets and understanding and ways of doing life. When you are an average swimmer and you start to get tired, you could easily slip into bad form and forget all of the technique you have learned. But when you have swum miles and miles everyday, even though you are pushing your body to it's absolute limits, there is no chance that you are going to slip into bad form when you are tired. You are so well trained the right technique has become your normal. This is what God requires of us—that the supernatural would become our normal. He wants us to be so well disciplined in spiritual practices that when the pressure is on and we are pushing ourselves to the absolute limits, there is no chance we will slip into bad habits in the natural.

This life will not make sense. You will not hear the applause of man when you start to build resource. If we are not strong in our spirit, we will not be able to live a life that requires us to operate in the spiritual realm. The truth is, we won't even see what God has for us unless we are looking with spiritual eyes and listening with spiritual ears. When we are training in the spiritual, we will be aware of an entirely new level of the world.

What God offers us, the Prada that He creates, cannot be purchased with anything this world can provide. No amount of striving, positioning, manipulating, or money can secure what God has. For athletes, they need to achieve a certain time to be eligible to compete in a race. This ensures that they are ready to be truly competitive and deserve to be there. How embarrassing it would be to run in a race that you clearly were not able to be competitive in. I love to watch the swimming in the Olympics and cheer really loudly to support those in the pool. I often look at the winners standing on the podium, and I become emotional as I imagine how amazing it must feel to stand and bask in the victory of that moment and what you have just achieved. But not for one moment would I ever want to actually stand on the blocks and compete against those swimmers. That would be terrible! They would finish 400m before I finished my first 50m.

Because there is such a level of resource needed to acquire the grand plans of God, it requires us to be qualified and ready to seriously take it on. Have you ever watched a preacher stand in front of a packed auditorium and smash an amazing word out of the park? Have you ever thought about how incredible it would be to preach God's word in that place and feel that sense of victory for the Kingdom? How would you do if you were thrust upon that stage right now? Have you trained to the point of being ready for that space? Don't wish that you could have what others have, until you have done what they have done to get there. It's immature to think we can have the end prize without putting in all the hard yards. Life doesn't work like that. No matter what it is God has for you, no matter what the Prada is in your life, God loves you too much to give it to you if you are not ready for it. That's why we have to produce the resource before we can take ownership of it. If we aren't willing to train, to earn the resource that is necessary to qualify, then we can window shop all we want, and look at others carrying their purchases. No matter how hard we wish, we will walk away empty handed. This isn't God being cruel or ruthless or mean, this is God being wise and loving and almighty.

It is only when we have trained spiritually that we have the level of resource to be able to make the dream a reality.

GOD PROMISES

When God wanted to speak the dream into Abraham, he took him out of the tent where he was. God stood Abraham under the stars and told him to look up. God wanted to show Abraham, right from the outset, that the promises He was about to show him and speak over him where only operational in the spiritual realm. These promises had no place in any space that Abraham could control or create. These promises were God's creation, and God planted Abraham in His creation to reveal them.

It was important for Abraham to be taken out of an environment where he felt confident and secure, and put into a landscape where he felt small against the backdrop of greatness across the skies. God needed Abraham to have a complete reliance on Him when taking on this covenant.

To further stress this point, God says to Abraham, "Count the stars, if you can…" God knew that Abraham had no hope of being able to count the stars in the sky. He wanted Abraham to know there were going to be many things about this journey he would not have an answer for. That no matter how long he stood under that sky, he would never be able to come up with the answer to that question, and that was ok. Abraham needed to be trained in such a way as to not have to have an answer for everything happening around him. Some things are part of the mystery of God, and as long as God is in control, we have nothing to be fearful of or anxious about. This is not an easy place to be. This stance takes courage and bravery. But we do not stand alone. We stand with the help of the Holy Spirit, who will continue to guide and strengthen us always.

Before we can take hold of the promises and destinies and covenants God has in store for us, He will take us out of the place where we feel comfortable and place us in environments, situations, and landscapes where we feel completely out of our depth. It is from this vantage point that God will continue to prove your inadequacy to be able to move forward in the natural in your own strength. It is only when we have total reliance, faith, trust, and obedience in Him that we will be able to see what He needs us to see and take hold of all that He has for us to carry.

My personal story is similar to this. God had a Prada for me and He needed me to be trained and operating in the spiritual, filled to the brim with resource so that I could take a hold of it, and walk carrying it in a way that would change the world. Just like Abraham, God took Stuart and I out of our normal environment and quite literally placed us under the stars to start speaking His destiny over us.

It was the Christmas of 2009. We had celebrated a wonderful holiday season with our family and friends, and continued the celebration over to December 26, which is my birthday. The night of December 26, we packed up our car with our two children, Madeline and Gabriel, and we headed off into the early hours of the morning to a beach on the South Coast of New South Wales in Australia. We were setting off for our annual camping vacation. Friends would be coming and going over the next two weeks, but we were setting up camp and staying put for the entire time. The days were long, the sun was hot, the water was crystal clear. It was the time of year where we completely stopped and refueled and immersed ourselves in the Word. We would rid our minds of busyness and distractions and wait on God for His leading for the coming year. We all loved this time. There was something magical about the days and breathtaking about the clear, quiet nights.

We were eating ice cream for breakfast, potato chip sandwiches for lunch, and drinking cold cans of Coke on the beach, listening to games of cricket on the radio. Friends had come and gone, and more were arriving soon. By some sort of chance (or so we thought at the time) we were going to be alone for New Years Eve. It would just be the four of us on the beach when the old year came to an end, and the New Year began. At first we felt disappointed that we would not have friends with us for the New Year celebrations, but then we felt blessed to have this time to savor for ourselves. Madeline and Gabriel were quite young at this point, and so after decorating our tents with streamers, adorning us all in glow sticks, and having some fun with sparklers, they fell asleep in a hammock together.

With a couple of hours still to spare before the clock struck midnight, Stuart and I decided to make ourselves comfortable in a hammock of our own. We pulled the hammock out from the tent, and set it up under the stars. We lay down together in that hammock, faces towards the night sky filled with stars, watching the fireworks randomly light up the sky, and we started to share our hearts with one another. We reflected on the year that was, and laughed and cried together about everything that had been. We then started to speak of the year ahead, and asked one another if God had said anything yet or hinted at any directions.

I almost felt silly sharing with Stuart. Something had been swirling around my mind for a few months, and I had not been able to make any sense of it. I felt an urge from God to speak out what was in my heart and tell Stuart these thoughts that I had been having. As we lay there together, both looking towards the heavens, I found myself telling Stuart that for some reason, New York City had been in my mind. There was a drawn out pause. All I could hear were the waves crashing in the distance, and the echoes of far-off fireworks exploding in the sky. When Stuart did speak, he changed our lives forever. He told me that he had been having the exact same thoughts. For whatever reason, New York City was in his spirit too.

We had no idea what was happening in that moment. We had no answers to give to one another. We lay there on that hammock under the vastness of a star-filled sky, and we vowed to God and to one another that we would follow Him wherever He was leading us. We acknowledged that He had placed New York City in our spirits, and we promised we would find out why.

It was in that moment, that night that God started to reveal to us His promise and calling over our lives. He had something so magnificent for us that He wanted us to be able to have it, not having to ever stop and ask how much was it going to cost. And so He orchestrated for us to be out under the starry night, just like Abraham. And just as Abraham could not count the stars that night, we had no answers to the questions that were already springing up in our minds. This was a journey that would not make any sense in the natural. This was a journey that would only work in the supernatural. This was a journey of epic proportions, definitely not for the faint hearted. This was a journey that would see us side by side, facing the unknown just the two of us. This was a journey that would require us to be vulnerable with one another and hold nothing back. This was a journey that would physically separate us from our friends and family and everything that we had ever known. This was a journey where we would leave the comforts of a life well-lived, and go into a space that would be stripped back to the bare essentials. We had a beautiful, large, fully-equipped home, with beautiful furniture and fixtures and outdoor spaces. But God took us away from all of that to a place where we camped, slept on stretcher beds, and cooked over a small gas cooktop, all to show us, and plant within us, a desire for our promise land.

What a prophetic picture of what God had in store for us. God works in rhythms and patterns and visions and dreams and whispers and images, and He was sowing into us an initial understanding of what He had prepared for us. The imagery of the richness of the skies set against the plainness of the campsite still takes my breath away. It wasn't about what we had, what we had acquired, or worked for, or could provide for our family, it was all about what He had. He had abundance so grand, so magnificent, it made our life's accumulation seem insignificant. He captivated us with a glimpse of the heavens, and nothing else could compare.

God ignited a taste for the Prada that night, and we have never been the same since. In our nothingness, we discovered His extravagance. Whatever it was that He was offering to us, we wanted it so badly we were willing to go after it with everything we had. We knew, more than ever before, we had to run these next steps with purpose in every step, building resource with every new day, being equipped to say, "Yes, that's the one I want, I'll take it."

2

SHOW ME THE MONEY

"I do not give to you as the world gives." John 14:27 (NIV)

One thing is certain with designer handbags— they never go on sale! These beauties are never subject to the normal discounts we can expect to see with other types of handbags. You will never walk down Fifth Avenue and see a sign in the front of Louis Vuitton that says, "50% off everything in the store." Imagine that! There would be chaos. Women would be falling all over themselves to get inside the doors. No, these handbags have a price associated with them, and you will pay that same price any day of the year. And strangely enough, this actually makes the process of buying one of these handbags a little easier. Knowing that you are not going to pay full price and then find them on sale next month eliminates a whole aspect of stress and concern at the time of purchase. There is never a situation where you regret spending the money you did, feeling like you have received a bad deal. The designers protect their customers in this way, shielding them from feeling anything but joy and thankfulness when they think about the purchase of their new handbag.

The dreams and destinies God has for us also never lessen in their value. There aren't some periods of the year where you can get a hold of them much easier than normal. There is a price to be paid, and this price is not subject to changing tides or whims. You don't commit to saying yes with the worry in the back of your mind that there could come a time when you could do this a lot easier. God would never want you to regret what you have sacrificed in order to take hold of what He was offering to you.

THERE ARE NO SUCH THINGS AS SHORTCUTS

There are no shortcuts in this process. If you want to own a Prada handbag, you have to have money to give to the sales assistant before you are permitted to leave the boutique. No money, no purchase. Sure you could be like the lady from the movie "Confessions of a Shopaholic," and charge everything to a credit card (or five). But eventually, no matter how long you try and defer the payment, you are going to be forced to come up with the money.

I find it interesting there is a business where women rent designer handbags. Instead of simply paying the price to own a handbag, they pay a significantly smaller amount in rent per month, and have a handbag to use for a limited period of time, before they need to hand it back or pay more rent. Some would say this is a sensible idea. But what are you really getting for your money? At the end of the week, month, year, what do you have to show for your investment? Sure, it may be less than what you would have paid if you had made the purchase, but buying the handbag means it is yours to keep. This bag becomes part of your identity. This bag helps you in your day to day. This bag can be handed down to your daughter or daughter-in-law or niece or friend. This is your handbag. It belongs to you.

Renting is a cop out. It's tasting the experience of owning a Prada handbag whilst considerably minimizing the risk, sacrifice, hard work, and decision making process. What do you really have to lose when you are simply renting? It will be fun for a season, and then you can hand it back. Renting is putting a safety net in place, making sure that you are going to be fine, not committing too much of your resource and yet getting what you want. If it ends up that you don't completely love the handbag, there is no harm done. You have lost a small amount of money, but can walk away and life will go on as normal. Renting is the ultimate attempt to have your cake and eat it too.

Understandably, it is the people who cannot afford to buy a Prada handbag outright that opt for renting. When it seems like the dream of ever owning a Prada is unattainable, renting is seen as a viable, second option. Instead of waiting and believing that you will eventually have the resource to be able to make the purchase, it is the taking-things-into-your-own-hands, quick-fix mentality. How the world loves this mentality. In our fast-paced, instant gratification society, we have come to believe that if it seems doubtful that we will get what we want, we simply do whatever it takes to get it now.

Sadly, this translates into so many other facets of life. If we can't find the man of our dreams, we either settle for a man that is pretty close or much worse still, we take someone else's man. Nothing breaks my heart more than to see women deliberately set out to take a man out of a marriage, because they haven't been able to get what another woman has been given. Women who entice married men away from their wives are selling themselves out of the sisterhood. We are women. We should be supporting one another, building one another up, looking out for each other and cheering each other on. At what point does it ever seem right to go behind other women's backs and steal, kill and destroy that which is most precious? The enemy has a field day when women go against other women.

I was shopping one day in NYC and I overheard two young women talking. One asked the other about a certain male co-worker. I heard the woman reply, "Oh, we're just friends, he's married." I was sickened to hear her friend reply, "So what? Who cares about that?" *Who cares? Who cares?* I wanted to turn around and give this young girl a piece of my mind. Of course I didn't. But I couldn't even look at her. I quickly left the store, feeling so sad and praying over the marriage I had just heard mentioned. *Oh Lord, please keep that marriage safe.*

It is this take-charge mentality that was the root of the very first sin. In the Garden of Eden Eve listened to Satan and ate from the tree of good and evil. She desired to get something, which seemed so hard and unattainable. When Adam and Eve ate that fruit, they gave authority to Satan. They gave him a foothold into the lives of mankind. They opened us all up to be born into sin and handed Satan an authority that was never meant to be his. There were dire consequences because Adam and Eve thought they could get what was only ever God's to give by their own means. Because a man had given that authority away, a man had to come and take it back. That is why Jesus came as a man, to take back the authority that had been wrongfully given to Satan. Jesus paid the ultimate price, the highest sacrifice, and gave his life to defeat the power of death once and for all.

I DID IT MY WAY

This pull within us to receive the promise in our own way, to make it happen so help us, is very real. Abraham, who was promised so much, fell victim to this mindset as well. God had promised Abraham he would be the father of many nations. He told him to look up into the sky and to see a heavenly perspective of the descendants that would be his. God had declared over Abraham his promises were coming, they would be a reality, he would receive them in their entirety. But instead of saying yes to God, giving his all and producing the required resource of faith, Abraham took a different approach. Just as Satan had used and manipulated Eve in the Garden of Eden, his hatred of women saw him target Sarah in this situation. The temptation came through Sarah, to ensure that they didn't miss out on receiving what God had for them. And instead of going through the full purchasing process, Abraham and Sarah came up with a quicker solution and conceived Ishmael with the maidservant Hagar.

The consequences of this decision are still felt to this day. Abraham's son Ishmael was not the promised son God had planned. Ishmael was the ultimate example of what the world can create.

And yet we see in this story that when Abraham did receive Isaac, the son that came from God's hand through his elderly wife Sarah, there was conflict between the two. The world's ways and God's promises cannot co-exist happily. You cannot create situations in your life, and expect those to fit in perfectly with the promises of God. God is a jealous God, and He will not share His affection with any other. You cannot sell out in some areas of your life and then expect peace and harmony to rule when you attempt to put it together with God's promises. Ishmael and Isaac were in conflict. The world's ways and God's ways were in conflict. To this day, conflict still rages in the Middle East stemming from these descendants of Abraham. And at the very heart and genesis of this battle is the way of God verses the schemes of man. This is a conflict that will never be resolved. This world is in a constant battle between good and evil. There are forces of good and forces of evil at work every day, all around us. And although Satan was defeated at the cross of Calvary, and death lost it's sting when Jesus rose from the grave, and the authority that Satan had enjoyed was taken from him forevermore, the battle still rages. Satan is not giving up. The world will never stop fighting to make its way *the* way. But Jesus is the way, he is the truth, he is the life.

We cannot see what God has for us and then come up with our own solutions about how to make the promises a reality. This mindset spells disaster not only in our lives, but also for the generations to come.

Once Abraham had repented for his sin and God had given to him his beloved Isaac, his ultimate Prada, we see an interaction that teaches us so much. God asked Abraham to go to the top of a mountain He would show him and sacrifice his son Isaac. We read that this was the final test of Abraham's faith. Why did God ask Abraham to do this? I believe God already knew what Abraham would do in this situation. The test was to reveal to Abraham himself how he would react. God needed to show Abraham that no matter what had happened in the past, he was now fully sold out and had all the resource needed to give to God to make the promises and plans come to pass. God wanted to prove that Abraham was totally reliant on Him and would never try to turn situations around in his own strength again, no matter how serious the consequences. Isaac was the ultimate promise of God to Abraham. Abraham loved his son more than anything else. He wanted him so badly. And yet, he was willing to kill Isaac, because he knew that if that was what God required, He would do it God's way. Abraham had so much faith to believe that God would accept his resource and give him Isaac. He said to the servants at the base of the mountain, "We will return in three days." Abraham knew even if he killed Isaac, God would somehow give Isaac back to him.

It was God who stopped Abraham from killing Isaac, and it was God who provided an alternative way. He produced a lamb caught in the bushes for Abraham to use as the sacrifice instead of Isaac. Abraham is celebrated as the Father of Faith because ultimately, he trusted God to set the situation and circumstances and did not intervene in his own strength. Abraham did not bow down to the world's ways of ensuring the promises were secure. He allowed God to have His way completely in his life, and he saw the fulfillment of all of God's promises because of it.

When we set aside our selfish ambitions, we will see God's

promises delivered to us in their entirety. God will hold nothing back from us when we give Him the resource of allowing Him to be fully in control. Satan is the father of lies and convinces us that unless we step in, we will never receive what God has shown us. And too often we give authority to this lie in our lives by taking authority away from God. This is a foolish way to live. I don't know about you, but I don't want what I can achieve. I want what God can give me. I know myself well. I know my limitations and my inadequacies. I look at what I can create, and then I get a glimpse of the universe that God has created. He wins. Hands down. Every time.

THE MINDSET OF SELF-RELIANCE

Another example of this can be found in the history of The Salvation Army. When we first arrived in New York City we heard a story about events that had taken place here many years ago. The founder's of The Salvation Army, William and Catherine Booth, had never accepted any money from the church or the government in funding what God had promised to them. The Salvation Army is a global denomination that was birthed in 1878 in England. It was 1852 when the founders William and Catherine Booth, driven by a passion to see people saved and lives transformed by Jesus, first started to walk the streets of London and preach the Gospel to the "whosoever". Booth put aside the conventional concept of church and pulpit and instead took his message to the people. He faced much opposition from other church leaders at the time, but this did not deter him from holding evangelistic meetings throughout England. It was 1865 when The Christian Mission was formally established. This mission evolved into The Salvation

Army by 1878. It was at this time that William Booth took on a military framework in running and managing the newly formed Army and the many outposts or Mission Stations operated with military uniforms, titles, and terminology. The first captain of The Salvation Army, a former chimney sweep name Elijah Cadman, is credited with instigating the wearing of the military-style uniforms after declaring at an early meeting, "I should like to wear a suit of clothes that would let everybody know I meant war to the teeth and salvation for the world." Catherine Booth designed The Salvation Army's flag, which displayed the Army's motto, "Blood and Fire." This indeed was a church on fire. With a foundation of the saving blood of Jesus, together with the power of the baptism of the fire of the Holy Spirit, The Salvation Army became a dynamic movement of the Evangelical Church that spread across the globe, and it was the Booth's Prada.

William and Catherine Booth remained faithful to the calling God had placed on them. They gave their lives to see God's plans and purposes come to fruition within The Salvation Army. God was faithful, and as He used them in this expression of the church, the Holy Spirit breathed upon it and it spread to the ends of the earth like wildfire. It was 1880 when members of The Salvation Army first arrived dockside at Battery Park, New York City. By 1928, Booth's daughter Evangeline was in charge of The Salvation Army. She allowed God to lead and therefore continued to have plenty of resource to receive the Prada's that God wanted to give to her and to this church. Evangeline was desperate to present the church in a more progressive light in New York City, and so in 1928 she contracted the most modern, cutting edge architectural firm to design a physical footprint to reflect the spiritual ground The Salvation Army occupied. And so, the historical Centennial Memorial Temple was built on 14th Street in New York City.

God had promised so much, and He was continuing to show The Salvation Army more of what was in store for them. But instead of continuing to rely on the supernatural element of God's hand alone, the story goes that Evangeline slipped into taking things into her own hands. The Social Services arm of The Salvation Army was growing in stature and influence. It was at this point Evangeline was tempted by an offer to secure substantial provision for outworking the vision of these services, without relying on the faith-based hand of God. Why would she doubt the God who had done so much and given so much? I cannot imagine how intense the pressure was for her at this time.

The US Government approached The Salvation Army in the United States and offered to provide funding for the Social Service programs offered. Never before had The Salvation Army accepted money from authorities or governments or any other body, rather they had relied totally on the hand of God to provide in ways of His choosing (mostly through personal donations from people moved by the heart and mission of The Salvation Army). Evangeline's attorney was reticent to offer his advice in this situation. He told Evangeline it would be better for her if she did not hear his words, because once she had knowledge she would be responsible for how she handled that knowledge. Evangeline rejected his warnings and asked for his advice anyway. Once pressed, he told her if she accepted this money from the government, she would be selling out to the world. He warned her there would be constrictions and limitations concerning the preaching of the gospel in these services if the money was coming from the government. He urged Evangeline not to accept the money.

Evangeline went against his advice. This was the first time The Salvation Army accepted money from an outside body. I believe Evangeline broke something in the spiritual realm over The Salvation Army. The total number of officers that were employed in full-time ministry at that time has never been surpassed. Likewise, the number of soldiers enrolled at that time has never been greater. The Salvation Army stopped growing and started maintaining. The world's ways and God's ways cannot co-exist. They cannot work in harmony with one another. Evangeline chose the world's ways, and we all live with the consequences today.

When we first arrived in NYC, we were upset to learn that many New Yorkers didn't know The Salvation Army was a church. For so many, The Salvation Army has its identity firmly planted in its Social Services, being known as a thrift store or a soup kitchen. There is very little recognition of The Salvation Army as the church of the living God. Coincidence? I think not.

I believe part of the calling that God has placed over Stuart and I, is about stepping into this space and taking back the authority, which was given away. Once The Salvation Army accepted funds from an outside body to assist in the provision of Social Services in New York, Salvation Armies all around the globe followed suite. It was in New York that the first authority was handed over, and the ripple effect was felt all around the world. God's plan is to take that authority back. Therefore, He is going back to the source of the original handover. New York City is where it started, and

New York City is where it will be won back. The ripple effect of this eminent victory is going to be felt all around the world. The Salvation Army will take back the authority that has been given to the world, and the church of The Salvation Army will rise up like never before. The original mantle and anointing will be brought to life, and The Salvation Army will take it's rightful place on the world stage as a church operating under the saving blood of Jesus, fueled by the fire of the Holy Spirit. The power and passion that was present in the early Salvation Army will see this church once again spread across the world and impact all nations as it hosts the presence of God.

The Centennial Memorial Temple on 14th Street is the platform from which we stand today. It's a building that represents the richness and fullness of the history of The Salvation Army coupled with a desire to change perception and present the message in a progressive, distinctive way, using master craftsmen and unusual materials.

We do not discount our heritage from The Salvation Army rather we lean into it and avail ourselves of the riches that lay within it. We hold onto the promise of scripture where God declares He is doing a new thing. The excellence and cutting-edge nature of The Centennial Memorial Temple, built under the supervision of the founder's daughter in the heartbeat of the most influential city in the world, is the most amazing position to be standing for God to build His church in The Salvation Army NYC.

The night before we attended our formal interview in the boardroom of the 14th Street, Greater New York Division of The Salvation Army, God spoke very clearly to both Stuart and I. We had been flown to New York City to meet with the leadership of the Greater New York Division about coming to take up full-time positions in ministering out of the main Centennial Memorial Temple. We caught up for lunch with two of the leaders who would be present at the interview the next day. They wanted to give us an initial idea of where they saw the boundaries lying. Through voicing their concerns about what would not be allowed or approved, Stuart and I got the distinct impression they were trying to prepare us for a scenario we had not imagined. We sat and listened to the rules, guidelines, and non-negotiables, interjecting often with questions and comments. Hilariously, all through these intense discussions we had a musician playing the piano in the restaurant we were having lunch in, and he continually kept asking us for song requests. We would be mid-sentence, and then turn and yell out a song title so the man would leave us alone and keep playing. It was classic New York!

As we were going our separate ways after lunch, the younger man stalled and waited back with me as I collected my things. He looked at me with such sadness in his eyes and said, "I'm so sorry. I'm sorry…" My heart felt so heavy.

Stuart and I went back to where we were staying and fell on our knees in prayer. We cried out to God to make a way through this seemingly Red Sea. We contacted friends in Australia and asked them to pray with us. It was an intense spiritual battle. Stuart and I went out for dinner later that evening, and as we sat outside on an Upper West Side pavement, I started to cry at the thought of not being permitted to come and take up this calling that God had placed on our lives. We were both so sad. We felt like we had seen the Prada bag, and had the resource we needed to purchase it, but the sales assistant was not going to let us take it.

It was at that moment that Stuart said he needed to share something with me. As we had been praying and seeking God all afternoon, God had spoken very clearly and directly to Stuart. He told Stuart he would be asked in the interview tomorrow what we wanted to be given by The Salvation Army. And when that question was asked, God told Stuart to say "nothing." God impressed into Stuart that he was not to ask for a thing from The Salvation Army, that God would provide all we needed to live and work in New York City. As soon as Stuart spoke it out, I immediately agreed with him. Yes, God had been whispering these same thoughts into my mind as we prayed that afternoon.

Stuart and I looked at each other from across the table that night, and agreed to trust God with our finances in a way we had never done before. It seemed crazy! I believe that was a defining moment right then. All of Heaven erupted in cheers at the witness of our commitment and resolve. God had repeatedly told us to be brave and very courageous in the months leading up to this moment. And although we had no idea why God was asking this of us, we knew He held it all in His hands, and He is forever faithful.

We sat in the interview the next day and saw God part the waters of the Red Sea before us, making a way where it seemed there wouldn't be a way. The Holy Spirit fell in that place and we were given the approval and authority to come and minister in this space and take a hold of the Prada God had been whispering to us. It was at this point the leader of The Salvation Army in The Greater New York Division picked up a pen and poised it over his notepad. "What do you want from us?" he asked. Bam! There was the question God told us would be asked. I looked at Stuart, and he spoke with authority and authenticity, like I have never seen. Stuart responded, "Nothing. We don't want anything." Everyone in the room looked at Stuart with a puzzled expression. Stuart continued, "Our children are in a wonderful private school in Australia. If you could help us with getting them into a private Christian school here in Manhattan, that would be awesome." And that was that.

We didn't know what God had planned for this situation. We had no idea how we would have the resource to be able to live in one of the most expensive cities in the world. But we knew if God had asked this of us, we had to be obedient and faithful to His instruction.

It wasn't until we had arrived in New York and taken up our positions within The Salvation Army that we learnt the story of Evangeline Booth. We were also fascinated to discover William Booth did not take any money from the church for his personal livelihood. Booth relied totally on God to provide funds for himself and his family. And how God did provide! God inspired Booth with the idea of a revolutionary invention. Booth invented and designed the Redhead matchsticks that we still use today. This one single God idea provided William Booth with more money than he could ever spend in his lifetime.

What an amazing testimony to the power and promise of God. No matter how attractive and secure the world's ways may seem, they are nothing in comparison to what God has for you. Again I'll say it: I chose God every time. I chose God's Prada over anything this world could ever offer.

NOT MY WILL, BUT YOURS BE DONE

How angry we must have made Satan that day when we refused to accept what he offered us financially in the boardroom of the wealthiest Salvation Army in the nation. How furious must he have been with us! We still are unsure about how God is going to provide for our ongoing financial needs. I don't write this from a position of already having the Booth "God idea" and receiving all the finances we could ever possibly need. But I do believe it is on the way. I declare that it is on the way! We have not taken matters into our own hands, and have not interfered with the plans of God. We have given God full control and thus we have built heavenly resource—enough resource to take that Prada bag without even having to ask how much it costs. We've paid the price, and now we will see that which God has destined for us coming into our hands. Glory to God!

When Jesus was baptized by John the Baptist, the Holy Spirit rested on his head like a dove, and God spoke over him from Heaven, "This is my son, with whom I am well pleased." It was in this moment that Jesus' ministry on earth started. He was identified and commissioned to go about his father's business. From his baptism, Jesus went into the wilderness and fasted for 40 days. It was during this time Satan came to tempt Jesus. It is important to note that in all of Satan's attempts to tempt Jesus, he tries to entice Jesus to take control of situations in his own strength as a man and deny God's control. In every circumstance, Satan is telling Jesus to step out and do what he can do in his own strength. Yes, Jesus could have done all three actions that Satan was telling him to do. He could have turned the rocks into bread, he could have commanded the angels to save him, he could have bowed before Satan—but he didn't. Jesus did nothing in his own authority. He was completely at one with God, and always forwent his will for his father's. If we are to be like Jesus, we must always forgo our will for God our Father's.

This was exemplified in the Garden of Gethsemane when Jesus paid the ultimate price and took his control of the situation completely away from himself. With the words, "Not my will but yours be done," Jesus became the lamb God had provided to Abraham to sacrifice in the place of Isaac. That lamb saved Abraham from losing his son. Jesus became the ultimate sacrifice and Savior for all who surrender to him and allow God to have full authority in their lives.

How arrogant of Satan to think he would be able to change the mind of Christ and lead Jesus into acting out of his own strength. And yet, why wouldn't he try? It had been so successful in the past, giving him some of his greatest victories. This scheme had brought down some of the greatest men ever to live: Adam, Abraham, and King David. Satan is not very creative. He comes to steal, kill, and destroy and he uses the same strategies over and over again to achieve this goal. Generation after generation within a family can all fall victim to the very same strategy of the enemy. If alcoholism brings father after father down in a family, great! Why would he ever need to change the strategy? That is why he is so outraged when a man rises up and breaks the curse of addiction in his family. The strategy is defeated, and Satan has to think up a new plan to bring the men of the generations down — to kill, steal, and destroy them.

If convincing people to create their own Ishmael's will steal, kill, and destroy their opportunity to have the resource needed for the Prada God has for them, then why change the strategy? It obviously works, because people all around the earth for generation after generation are falling for this lie and scheme.

I was driving in my car one evening, heading to a board meeting. I had been in prayer that day, seeking God's heart and asking for specific direction. It had been several months since we had heard anything from the leadership in The Salvation Army New York, and we were desperate to hear that progress was being made on establishing our positions in the ministry. As I was driving and being still before God, a thought came into my mind so strongly. I heard God say, "Don't make an Ishmael." *What?? What does that even mean?* I wanted to dismiss the thought by shrugging it off, "That's weird," but God impressed it again to me. "Don't make an Ishmael." I agreed and in that moment, I promised Him I would not make an Ishmael. I had no idea how I would even try and do such a thing, but nevertheless I stood and made the resolve in my spirit before God.

I shared with Stuart what had happened, and we wrote it in our prayer diary – just in case —and moved on. It wasn't long after that my spiritual mentor asked me about New York. She suggested contacting them and putting some pressure on the situation. I explained to her I had promised God I would not make an Ishmael, and that trying to push The Salvation Army New York into a decision was taking matters into my hands. Maybe that was why God had spoken to me about this very point, so I would know not to push things from my end.

But it wasn't until something came across my computer screen not long later that I knew what God was speaking to me about that night in the car. At the time we had first heard God's calling about New York City, there were two Australian expressions of the church starting out in New York City. Both of these churches were from a church that had mentored us from afar, and that we felt a very spiritual affinity to. On our first visit to New York, we tried to see if God was wanting us to come alongside what He was doing in these other two young churches. God closed doors to both.

We had long since moved on from this idea, knowing that this was not part of God's plans for us and New York. But we had followed the development of these churches very closely, and constantly prayed for them, and supported them financially, and any other way we could from so far away.

It was from one of these churches that I saw an advertisement for a ministry position. The position was for pastors of their upcoming Brooklyn campus. As I read down the criterion that was desired for the pastoring couple, I started to check off every point. Yep, yep, yep, check, check. Everything listed was everything Stuart and I were. This job description could have been tailor made for us. The last item was for the successful couple to have a genuine love for New York City and the people in it and a desire to see God move in that place.

Instantly my mind went wild. We could apply for this! We could go to New York City and be a part of this amazing, dynamic church that was an exact fit for us! We would be able to have the dream of living and ministering in New York City. We would be able to have the promises God had spoken over us. We could do this! This could totally happen!

And just like that, I remembered the promise I had made to God. "I will not make an Ishmael." This was my Ishmael. This was my temptation to sell out on God and take matters into my own hands. This was the situation that could destroy my resource and leave me coming up short to receive the Prada that God had for us.

Did I want what I could make happen, or did I want the full promise of God and whatever His plan was? Even though I still had no idea how it was all going to work, I knew that it would, in His way. I chose God.

Make mine Prada… Every time!

3

I NEVER DID CARE FOR FANCY PACKAGING

"Look at the lilies and how they grow. They don't work or make their clothing, yet Solomon in all his glory was not dressed as beautifully as they are. And if God cares so wonderfully for flowers that are here today and thrown into the fire tomorrow, he will certainly care for you." Luke 12:27-28 (NLT)

There was an advertisement on Australian television a couple of years ago. It was advertising the base or home brand of a major Australian supermarket. This brand was typically known as a no frills, no fuss, cheaper option to other leading brands. The advertisement showed a woman standing in her kitchen, looking out of the window at her husband. He was a plain looking man—just going about his everyday chores around the house. The advertisement ended with her standing next to her husband and hugged him saying, "I never did care for fancy packaging." It used to make me laugh every time I watched it.

Sadly, the idea of not wanting anything fancy is all too common in certain groups of people within society. It is usually those who have suffered so many disappointments and setbacks in life they become afraid to hope for something better.

I can hear some women saying to me now, "I could care less for a Prada handbag. My handbag is just fine. Who needs a Prada?" My response back to them would be, "Ain't nobody got time for that attitude!" What is it with this train of thinking? I do not want to dismiss the hardships and struggles of so many people, or diminish how hard life can be. But I don't want to celebrate it either. You can focus on all the bad stuff in life, or you can chose to change your focus.

We are all able to focus on the good, because we all have the same opportunity to follow Jesus. Jesus is the reason why people can look beyond their present circumstances and hope for a better day. The Proverbs 31 woman "laughs with no fear of the future" (Proverbs 31:25). How do we look at the days to come and laugh rather than fear? We place our hope in Jesus. We lift our eyes to look into the face of Jesus. We open ourselves to our Savior, Jesus. And we hear and believe the promises of God over our lives.

When we are looking forward and not backward, when we are focusing on His strength and not our own weaknesses, when we receive His forgiveness and let it flow through us to those who have hurt us, when we are honest with our feelings and ask God to help us deal with whatever is there, when we don't instantly dismiss the greatness God has planned for our life—we will see the

Prada, and want it so badly we live our lives in a way that builds the resource to be able to get it.

The truth is, the devil does not want you to walk through life carrying all that a Prada bag represents. He doesn't want you to have God's big-ticket items. He doesn't want you to experience all that it will mean to not only your life, but also all of those in your world. Why? Because he can't have it! And if he can't have it, then he definitely does not want you to have it. He knows all too well the treasure that lies within such God plans and promises, and he will tell you anything to make you reject it.

Part of the scheme of the enemy is trying to convince you that you don't want such extravagance from God, you don't need it, and you could care less about it. He is the father of lies, and he lies to you constantly. But when we let the light of God illuminate our life and see Jesus, who is the truth, our perspective on God's extravagance changes.

A POVERTY MENTALITY

Sadly, in many Christian circles, a lack or poverty mentality is thought more holy and God-honoring than a wealth mindset. Dr. Ruby Payne, in her book *Understanding a Framework of Poverty,* presents her research on the different class experiences (poverty, middle class, wealth) and explains the different levels of mindsets and characteristics attributed to each one. There is nothing God-honoring about constantly living with a poverty mindset. It is a mindset that focuses on survival and holding tight onto anything that comes your way. Dr. Payne described in her research that when you hold a poverty view you believe in the notion of fate, and think you are powerless to change much.

There is a victim mentality linked with poverty, where anxiety, limitation, and resentment are felt towards God because He is not changing your circumstances. The gospel is powerless and life in God is not supernatural. When you have a poverty mindset you are not thinking Prada.

Heaven is filled with Prada bags people convinced themselves they couldn't have. How sad it must be for God to look at hurting hearts that refuse to take hold of the inheritance and richness that has been planned and purposed for their lives. In Jeremiah 29:11 it says, "For I know the plans I have for you," declares the Lord, "They are plans for good and not for evil. To give you a future and a hope." God's plans for your life will give you hope. The more hopeless you feel in yourself, the more you need to lean into God and go after the plans and purposes He has destined for you, because it will bring hope to your life like nothing else will. And when you have hope, you have the strength to go after the Prada. Because no matter how dire the situation looks in the present, there is the hope that a new day is coming.

At the very heart of it all, people convince themselves they do not want God's Prada, because their fate has determined they don't deserve it. Too many people ask themselves, "Why should someone like me ever expect to have something like that?" The deeply personal sense of powerlessness and rock bottom self-esteem, demand that eyes remain looking downward, and those fanciful thoughts of a better life are quickly snuffed out. If you think you are never going to be eligible for something, how can you ever believe God has greatness for you?

You are precious to God. He loves you. He created you. He formed you and knew you when you were in your mother's womb. He has created greatness for you, because He believes you are worth it. Choose to block out the voices that would tell you otherwise. Listen instead to the voice of God. He will tell you who you are, and what you mean to Him. He will tell you He can forgive you for everything you have ever done and cast it away as far as the east is from the west. He will remember it no more. He will tell you that He has so much in store for you.

YOUR INHERITANCE

God has given you an identity. You may not know who you are, but God does. You are the child of a King. You were worth sending His son to die for. And you are worth the very best Heaven has to offer. Your value is beyond measure. When God sees you, He doesn't see what you see. He looks past your outward appearance and all the other periphery, and instead looks at your heart. You were created in His image. You are capable of carrying all that He has for you to carry. He created you to be strong, loving, faithful, brave, and kind. He created you to add something beautiful to this world. He created you to worship Him.

The truth is, it is only when we hand our lives and circumstances over to God that we not only have the resource we need to take hold of the big items, but we have the belief and desire to go after them in the first place. When we are in control of our lives, there will always be doubt in our spirit about whether we are in a position where we could ever have this, and whether we could ever achieve it. When God is in control of our lives, when

He is given the rightful place in our hearts, we know who we are. We understand our position and worth, and we know there is a limitless inheritance and resource waiting for us to access from a God who is more powerful than we can possibly imagine. How different these two mindsets are. They have the power to bring life or death to any person.

Jesus said he came so that we may have life, life in all its fullness. The life Jesus came to give you is a life filled with Prada. It's a life filled with the plans, purposes, destinies, and inheritance of a God who knows no limits. This is living. There is nothing of lack in this life, because God does not operate in lack. He owns the cattle on a thousand hills, He spoke the world into existence, He has a kingdom of riches and glory. God never thinks small. He never thinks temporary. When He set the sun in the sky and the earth on it's axis, He did it to last. And when He created you, He did not do so in lack. There is nothing lacking within you to be all that God created you to be and live the life He created you to live. There may have been things stolen from you. You may have had your childhood stolen, or your joy, or trust, or finances, or confidence, or your marriage. But whatever you have had stolen, I want to tell you it doesn't rule you out of the game. It doesn't disqualify you. Jesus died on the cross so that you can have the power to take back everything the enemy has ever stolen from you. Don't live as though you are defeated. Live in the power and victory and freedom given to you by Christ Jesus.

GOD'S EXTRAVAGANCE

When you know God, you know His extravagance. It is part of

the very nature of who He is. He didn't place a few stars in the sky. He placed billions of them. One of my favorite things to do when we are out of the city is to look up into a night sky. We were sailing a catamaran around the Whitsunday Islands in the Great Barrier Reef in Australia. It had been a really tough trip and Stuart and I were fishing off the back of the boat late one night, trying to relax and unwind. It seemed there was one thing after another going wrong, all out of our control. At one point, I looked up. It literally took my breath away to see the sky in all of its magnificence. The stars were incredible. I felt like I could see right into the Milky Way. What extravagance was on display for us to enjoy. It was a message to us that night: No matter what earthly problems and limitations we may face in this world, we serve and love a God who knows the limitlessness of a night sky like the one before us. We didn't have to try and control our environment, because if He can control the night sky, He can control our little world.

God moves in extravagance. It's how He rolls! To limit His extravagance over your life is to limit the full measure and portion of what He has for you. I don't know about you, but when I am the recipient of someone's extravagance, I want to do anything I can to give something back to him or her. If someone is extravagant with their encouragement and praise, I want to encourage them and praise them. If someone buys me beautiful gifts, I make sure I have extra special thought and consideration when buying them gifts. If someone is extravagant in their time for me, I want to be more available for them when they need it.

When God gives to me so much, and extravagantly pours out His love, grace, mercy, and forgiveness over me, I want to give Him my extravagance. You can't receive all that God has for you without being compelled to give Him all you have. And even though what you give to Him is so precious, and so valuable, and so costly, you will never out-give God. He is no man's debtor, and we can never give Him more than He has given to us.

Therefore when we fully know God, and we understand and experience His extravagance, we will be compelled to give Him our all, give Him control. This does not leave us poorer, but rather builds the very resource we need to take a hold of the destinies and promises and inheritance that we cannot even dream or imagine. How amazing is God's economy? He doesn't operate on the same economic scale as the world. His values are different.

THE FRAGRANCE OF WORSHIP

One of my favorite stories in the bible is the story of a woman who came to a house where Jesus was and poured out expensive perfume all over his feet. This woman walked right into the environment of that house and knelt at Jesus' feet. She took a small bottle of perfume that was worth around a year's wages, and broke it open, anointing the feet of Jesus with it. As she covered his feet with this sweet perfume, she wept and dried his feet with her hair. The other men in that house were indignant at her actions, calling her extravagance wasteful and unnecessary. They were adamant the woman could have put the money the perfume was worth toward much better causes. But Jesus felt the opposite. He called her extravagance worship. Placing worth on our King. And he told those opposing her, namely Judas Iscariot and the other Pharisees, wherever the story of the gospel was spoken, so too would the story of what the woman had done for him would also be shared.

I love this. What is Jesus saying? He is saying that not only is it ok to be extravagant towards him, but extravagance will always be linked to the gospel. Not just his extravagance to us, but our extravagance to him. He celebrated what that woman brought to him that day, and challenged the men in the room about what they had done for him in comparison. This story gives us powerful insight into the heart of Jesus. He wants us to know and understand how to be extravagant to him. He wants us to know that it is not wasteful, or shameful, or misdirected.

He wants us to see what extravagance does to the one who is giving. The woman that day broke open the bottle of perfume, used her hands to rub it in, and then her hair to dry Jesus' feet. She would have had that perfume all over her. In fact, she probably walked away having more of the scent on her than Jesus had on him. That is such a truth of the character of God. He never lets us give to Him, and then walk away unchanged. The woman didn't walk back out of that house smelling the same. She walked out covered in the smell of expensive perfume. She walked out different. When we pour our extravagance over God, we will be changed. We can't help but be affected. That is how the Kingdom of God works. Extravagant worship will fill you with more than you have given God.

But my favorite part of this story is the one verse at the end of the story (John 12:3), which simply says, "The fragrance filled the whole house." Yes! How amazing is that! This house! The house of a Pharisee, the house filled with negativity and naysayers and people opposed to what she was doing. This space, this environment, this atmosphere was filled with the sweet fragrance of her extravagance. It affected them all. There is power in your worship. There is power in your extravagance. Because one woman was brave enough to come into a place and bow at the feet of Jesus and give, the whole house was affected.

Not only will your extravagance benefit your life, it will affect the lives of all around you. Your family and friends and co-workers and school mates and everyone else that God has placed in your influence, will be affected because you came to Jesus and gave him your best, your extravagance. Their lives will be richer because of what you have sown.

The world will try and tell you that you have misplaced your extravagance. They will call you wasteful, and inappropriate, and unnecessary. But God looks at you and what you bring, and He calls it worship. He links it with His gospel that says, "God so loved the world, that He gave His one and only son, so that whosoever believes in Him will not perish but have everlasting life." Now that's extravagance!

There is power in the gospel to change your life and give you an eternity in Heaven. There is power in extravagance to change the lives of other people, and give them an eternity in Heaven.

MAINTENANCE MODE

There is no power in maintenance. You may not suffer from a lack mentality, but you may struggle with the temptation to maintain. How easy it is for this temptation to take a grip on you and seriously limit what God can do with your life. The world cries out to you to be happy with what you have. Keep the status quo. Don't tempt fate. The grass is never greener on the other side. Don't use energy you don't have. All the while, all of Heaven is screaming out for you to go for it! Be brave and very courageous, jump in, get out of the boat! Your best days are still in front of you — don't settle for anything less than the dream.

As hard as it can sometimes be, if you go into maintenance mode in life, you'll never take a hold of the Prada. It just doesn't work that way. God loves us way too much to let us stay the same. He is constantly doing a new thing in and through you. No matter what you have achieved in His name, He has bigger days planned ahead. You are on this earth for a reason. "Live a life worthy of the calling placed upon you…" God never called anyone to be ordinary, or average, or safe. He created us for greatness and created you for a purpose that is impossible to achieve without Him.

The moment you say to yourself that life is good, there are no real complaints, everything is going along nicely enough… It's time to panic! This is a sign that you have slipped into maintenance mode, and it will take everything you have within you to hold onto God and let Him pull you back out. Maintenance mode does not provide you the resource for Prada! You need to be in the faith zone, not the maintenance zone.

When resource is tight, and you just have enough to make ends meet, the last thing that you are thinking of is a designer label. Designer doesn't even enter the equation when you are living from paycheck to paycheck and you are spending down to your last few dollars every two weeks. If you have the essentials, that is awesome! You are keeping your head above water, and always looking forward to the next payday. You are not going out shopping for a

Louis Vuitton, Chanel, or Prada anytime soon. That is just an impossible dream.

How similar this is to our spiritual lives. If we are just going through the basics with God, ticking off all the essentials of Christian day-to-day life—reading the bible, praying, giving our tithes, but really only just living from Sunday to Sunday—the big things God has in store for us will not even enter the equation. When your head and heart are in the mode of maintaining, they are not in the zone for dreaming. When you are thinking survival, you are not thinking abundance. How hard it is to rise up and think about the days that lie before you when you are so fixated and focused in the day-to-day.

I have seen people walk into church on a Sunday morning, week after week, at the exact same marker in their race. They have made it again to another Sunday, ready to be filled up so they can get through another week. By the grace of God they will be here next week, for another infilling, so they can make it through the week after that. It's like Groundhog Day! No wonder they look so exhausted, it's like mice running around, spinning on the wheel. There is plenty of movement happening, but no ground being taken.

That's what maintenance mode will do to you. It will exhaust and drain you, but limit you from taking any real ground. Sure, you haven't gone backwards, but you haven't gone forward either! You are no real threat to anyone, especially the devil, because you are so predictable. He always knows where to find you, maintaining what you already have. All across the world, the devil is keeping Christians busy maintaining the life that God has given to them.

He'd rather see you in a heap on the ground, but seriously this is the next best thing. He writes off the collateral damage being done in the small stuff because it means you won't go near the real game-changing things God would love you to take hold of. Obviously the best-case scenario for the devil is if you become so exhausted maintaining the life you already have you fall in a heap and can't even do that anymore.

Where are you focusing your energy? Where is your time, talent, faith, expectation, belief, and perseverance going? Are all your efforts used up in maintaining the life you already have—refining it, tweaking it, filling it with more of the same? Or do you reserve your efforts and energy for the greatness of those dreams, destinies, and inheritances God houses for us, just waiting for us to take hold of them with a level of resource that is more than enough?

It is very easy in the Christian world today to be in maintenance mode. People will encourage you, support you, and celebrate you when you are maintaining all that is on your plate. You will be seen to be doing an amazing work, and others will love to see you excelling in the life you lead. There is nothing bad about this. The danger comes when there is maintenance alone. There has to be a balance. Sure, you have to steward well all that God has given to you, but you also must not let it hold you back from going after the big ticket items!

When you step out of maintenance mode in your relationship with Jesus, you will have the energy for more. You will walk into church every Sunday different from how you were the last week. People will see changes in you all the time. You will not plateau, you will not burn out, you will not become stale, because you will be constantly striving to take new ground, build more resource, and carry the very best of what Heaven has to offer.

The people I look up to are not the people who are maintaining in life, but the people who are constantly looking over the bar, up into the abundance. I love to watch people who do life with a zeal and zest for the impossible, for the hard to come by, for the exclusive and superb.

We recently were on vacation at Disney World in Florida. I love being at Disney World. It didn't get its reputation for being the happiest place on earth for no reason. The heart of Disney is that dreams come true. We sat in a theatre amidst the fun and wonder of amusement park rides, and watched a short film on Walt Disney himself. What an amazing man, what an inspiration! Here was a man who never fell into the trap of maintaining. He always saw more, dreamed more, hoped and imagined for more. He came to a point in his life where through some business matters that had gone terribly wrong, he had lost everything he had worked for up until that point.

Most people would have gone into maintenance mode right then and there, trying to protect and maintain whatever they had left. Not Walt Disney. He sat on the train leaving Manhattan at a defining point in his life. It was in this space he started to draw, and as he drew, he created Mickey Mouse. Who would have ever thought one drawing of a mouse could have lead to the empire that is Disney today? And yet it did. But it so easily could have been over as soon as it started.

In one of his darkest moments, sitting on that train next to his wife, Walt Disney picked up a pencil and started to draw again.

He could have easily sat there and wallowed in his sorrow and self pity, but he picked up his pencil yet again. And when the drawing came, he didn't hold it so tightly it never had room to breathe. Walt Disney did not maintain Mickey Mouse; he opened himself completely to take it to heights and depths beyond his imagination.

RESTLESS FOR A REASON

God honors our persistence. He honors our bravery when we do not let past failings stop us from trying something new. He wants us to take up the very things He has placed in our hands, even though they may have failed us or have been taken from us in the past. Do not be forever sidelined because there have been times when things haven't worked. Where there has been past failures and disappointment, don't give up. Keep going. Pick up the pencil again.

God also honors our faith and belief for more. A drawing can stay a drawing, or it can become a Disney. The choice is yours. Will you hold on so tightly, maintain so thoroughly, and keep protected so vigilantly that there is no space for growth? Just as God gave each one of us free will so we can grow into all He ever dreamed we could be, so too we have to allow the dreams God places in our hands to grow into all that they can be.

I will never forget an anniversary dinner Stuart and I shared when we were in our late twenties. There was a beautiful restaurant on the water in our hometown of Newcastle. It was the type of place you would go, and your table was your table for the night. No one was coming in after you, and none was before you. You had the whole night to sit and watch the sunset and talk into the night. Our wedding anniversary is in February, so the weather in

Australia was always warm. Stuart would reserve a table out on the deck over the water, and we would dress up and head out for a wonderful night. Our meals would come out slowly and gradually over the course of the evening, and drinks would be intermittently served between courses. The sounds of the water lapping against the piers could be heard so quietly in harmony with the soft tones of music. It was an ideal setting and if I close my eyes even now, I can still picture us sitting there.

This one particular anniversary dinner, I felt heaviness in my spirit as we started to share. I had one of those moments where there were so many right things in my life, and yet I felt such a longing for more. I'm not sure if you have ever felt this, and it really is quite difficult to articulate, but I knew there was more I wanted to be doing with my one and only life.

As I poured out my heart to Stuart and told him how I was feeling, he listened and leaned into me from across the table. His eyes looked intently into mine with a love and understanding that made it so much easier to let it all go. I started to weep as I suddenly felt with every fiber of my being that I was missing something. I didn't just want the average, I wanted the above and beyond.

I had the most amazing husband in the world, I had my precious daughter Madeline, I had my loving family, beautiful friends, fulfilling ministry, a secure job in a wonderful Christian school. I had so much! There would have been many people who looked at my life and would have given anything to have what I had. And even though I was thankful for all God had given to me, there was a restlessness I believe came from Him, a stirring to not settle and maintain. A call was inside of me to keep going, keep pursuing, keep pushing, and dreaming, and planning, and scheming in Jesus' name.

In Genesis 12 we see the start of the story of Abraham (called Abram at that point). The first heading is titled, "God promises a nation to Abram." What an amazing way to start a story! But I am forever taken with the last verses of the preceding chapter. Genesis 11 verse 31-32 talks about Abram's father, Terah. It reads, "Terah took his son Abram, his daughter-in-law Sarai, and his grandson Lot (his son Haran's child) and left Ur of the Chaldeans to go to the land of Canaan. But they stopped instead at the village of Haran and settled there. Terah lived for 205 years and died while still at Haran."

There is sadness when I read these verses. This is a picture of a life that was meant to go somewhere, but it never got there. Terah was headed to the land of Canaan, but instead he settled at the village of Haran. He settled! Terah lived and died and settled without seeing the full promise of the land that God was leading him to. It was then his son that God raised up and took further and promised a nation to. Oh, may my life never settle short of where God has destined me to be. No matter how nice it is, how comfortable it may be, how friendly everyone there is, how popular the spot, never settle anywhere short of where God has told you to go.

The restlessness in your spirit is there for a reason. It's to make sure that you don't settle! If you are restless, then you are going to continue to search for more. As soon as you become too comfortable and start to maintain what you have, it is too easy to end the journey right where you are.

That night at dinner with Stuart, God was stirring within me restlessness to ensure I didn't settle where I was. As great as it was, there was more ground for me to take. It wasn't where my story ended. I didn't know where my story ended, I had no idea what the future looked like, but I knew that it wasn't time to sit down. There were places to go, people to see, lives to change. And although I felt quite distressed by my hunger for more, I also felt a strange peace knowing God was in control and He never did anything small.

A few years went by after that night, and although I continued to live out every day to the full and step into all that He had given to me, I forever had this underlying ache. It never left me. It was always there. I had tried to see if I could determine what the more looked like quite a few times over these years, but always ended up with a closed door or a resounding heavenly no. Every time I did try a door, I made people in my world very nervous. People around me didn't want anything to change. In fact they would have loved for me to settle right where I was. But I couldn't settle. I needed to keep moving.

So when God first placed that initial "Mickey Mouse drawing" into my hands, of New York City, it was a defining moment. Was I brave enough to try this door and see if it would lead to more of what God had in store? Or would this door cause more pain and anguish for those around me? I let the thoughts God was placing in my mind about New York City sit and breathe, as I pondered them and considered them and thought them through. So when Stuart and I were laying on a hammock that New Years Eve, I decided that it was the time to try the door. I didn't let the past's failings and defeats stop me from taking this step yet again. And to my joy and wonder and excitement, when I spoke out my thoughts, revealed the "drawing" to Stuart, he showed me the same back!

What a way for God to confirm this was the way He wanted us to journey. He is so amazing! It wasn't a matter of Stuart agreeing to go along with my thoughts, or me going along with his thoughts. He gave the same thoughts to us both so we could instantly know this was different and this was of Him. Oh how He loves us!

More than that, just as Walt Disney could have seen the drawing of Mickey Mouse, but never have pursued it or given his life to making it all that it has become, Stuart and I could have heard that initial call to New York City but never have done anything about it. We lived a comfortable life. We lived ten minutes from my parents and my brother and his family, and saw them all every other day. We had a successful financial planning business that provided us with a great amount of income and the flexibility to lead ministries. We had a beautiful home, our children were in a fantastic Christian school, we all had so many friends that were like family, we were able to give significantly of our finances and time to those in our world. Life was good. In fact, it was very, very comfortable. It could have been so easy to adopt the mindset that this will be just fine. And instead of going all the way to Canann, just making a nice life at Haran.

Praise God we didn't! Don't get me wrong, there is a lot to miss about our old life, but at the end of the day, nothing compares to doing the very thing you know you were created to do. Nothing compares to Prada!

4

YOU CAN TELL IT'S A FAKE

"Knowing the correct password – saying 'Master, Master,' for instance – isn't going to get you anywhere with me. What is required is serious obedience – doing what my Father wills. I can see it now – at the Final Judgment thousands strutting up to me saying, 'Master, we preached the message, we bashed the demons, our God-sponsored projects had everyone talking.' And do you know what I am going to say? 'You missed the boat. All you did was use me to make yourselves important. You don't impress me one bit. You're out of here.'" Matthew 7:21-23 (The Message)

Imitation, reproduction, copy, fakes—whatever you want to call them, there are tons of these designer handbags on the market today. Banking on the fact there are many, many women who would love a designer handbag and yet haven't got the resource to buy one, companies generate fake handbags to sell as the real thing, thus providing a solution for women all over the world. It's big business. Even though it is illegal to sell these handbags, passing them off as something they are not, it doesn't seem to stop either the sellers or the buyers. Brazen sellers on the streets of New York lay down a rug with all of the copy handbags sitting on top. If there is any hint of authorities in the immediate area, the seller simply grabs the corners of the rug, scooping up all of the bags at once, and takes off!

Soho was an area in New York City where fake handbags were notoriously sold. If you wanted a good, imitation designer handbag, you would head straight to Soho. There you would be able to purchase a copy of your favorite handbag for a fraction of the price. It was a hotspot for women and a haven for lies and deception. Authorities moved into this arena in Soho, and closed down all of these fake handbag businesses. There was a massive clearing out in the neighborhood of all things fake. Now when you head down to Soho, instead of finding stores selling fake Prada handbags, you will find the authentic Prada flagship store! The fake outlet has been replaced with the flagship. Any ground the imitators attempted to take has not only been reclaimed, but the designers have now added the flagship store in a beautiful statement of victory.

RECLAIMING GROUND

The kingdom of lies and deceit is continually trying to take new ground. But a new day is dawning, and a fake, empty gospel is no longer going to cut it. It is time to take back territory and reclaim it for God. It is time to present the world with the authentic gospel and love of Jesus that will satisfy even the hungriest of hearts. And God will honor this not only with a small outlet for His designs, but a flagship! That is my prayer for The Salvation Army New York

City. As we take back the ground the enemy has stolen, we will see an outpouring of God through The Salvation Army over New York City like never before. We will stand in the grandeur of the flagship and herald an awakening of all things magnificent.

God promises He will work all things together for good for those who know and trust in Him. I love this promise. I live by this promise. I claim it and believe it always. The impostors set out to profit from the true designers and undermine the entire designer handbag industry. But in a beautiful ironic twist, they have only added to the landscape and popularity of the designer handbag environment. Renee Richardson Gosline discovered in her doctoral thesis that after owning a fake Prada handbag, women would crave the real thing. They'd abandon their imitation copies and invest in a real Prada. The very strategy used to woo women was the very thing propelling them more intensely away from the fakes and towards the authentic.

The enemy may be trying to woo us into a counterfeit gospel that we can have without the price tag attached. But instead of taking people away from the Kingdom of God, the more fake the gospel and expression we experience, the more we crave the real thing. We become more desperate than ever to hold the very real and authentic promises of God in our hands, and we will do anything to have them and to experience God's outworking power and glory.

When asked about his greatest fear for the church of this century, William Booth's first words were, "Religion without the Holy Spirit." The enemy has had his time of selling religion devoid of the presence of the Holy Spirit. But after having a taste of it, we are universally unsatisfied. The church all across the globe has poetically been propelled towards a desire for a real and tangible experience of religion that is based in relationship and has the mark of the maker all over it.

THE SHINE SOON FADES

Before I ever owned a real designer handbag, I first owned a fake designer handbag. I was with my family on holidays in Fiji. One night we went for a look through the main market area, and we stumbled across some fake Louis Vuitton handbags hanging up at the back of a clothing store. More than anything else in that store, these handbags caught my eye. Stuart followed my intense gaze, and told me to ask for a closer look. The sales assistant lifted one of the handbags down for me, and I looked over it. After being told the reasonable price of the handbag, Stuart assured me that if I wanted to buy it, I should go ahead. I had never held a Louis Vuitton handbag before, but from what I could gather, if this was an imitation, it was a great one. This handbag looked exactly the same as any Louis Vuitton I had seen in magazines or photos. So I went ahead and purchased the handbag in the chocolate brown, signature Louis Vuitton style. I wasn't definite about whether it was a fake, but I kind of thought it must be.

I was feeling great about my handbag purchase. In fact, my new Louis became my handbag of choice. I would take it everywhere. It matched with all of my outfits, and was a perfect fit for my lifestyle. I loved it. I loved having it hanging off my arm. That is, until one fateful day. We had been in Sydney, and were on the way home to Newcastle. We had stopped for a bathroom break at the service stations. As I was about to walk out of the bathroom, three Asian ladies walked in. Immediately, their handbags caught my eye. Each one of them had a beautiful designer handbag hanging on their shoulder. As I looked again, more closely this time, I saw my handbag, sort of. What I saw was the authentic version of what my handbag was modeled from. If there was any doubt in my mind about whether my handbag was a fake, it was gone in that moment. I knew without a shadow of a doubt the handbag I was holding was definitely NOT a Louis Vuitton original.

I must have looked like a deer in the headlights! I just stood there, staring at this lady's Louis Vuitton bag. I was mortified, upset, and embarrassed, all at the same time. Once I had semi composed myself, I tried to get out of that bathroom as quickly as I could. I was angling myself, trying to hide the handbag over my shoulder, praying that none of these women would see it as I made my hasty exit. I could not stand to have my poor excuse for a Louis in the same space as the real deal. It was just too confronting and humiliating. I mean, it was really bad, on so many levels.

I got home that day, emptied all of the contents out of my Louis Vuitton-ish handbag, and never used it again. I vowed I would never buy another designer copy handbag again. I had learned my lesson. I never wanted to feel ever again the way I felt in the bathroom that day.

My handbag was great until it was in the same space as the real deal. And then there was nothing great about mine at all. The shape was slightly out of alignment, the color was darker, the zips were the wrong color, the leather trims were different, the label was in the wrong place. I mean, it was amazing how wrong my handbag really was. Now imperfections I had never seen or noticed before became so glaringly obvious to me, I couldn't look anywhere else. In one short encounter, I knew that my handbag was never going to be the same to me ever again. It was ruined for life. I just couldn't bear the thought of taking hold of it ever again.

Tragically, many people opt for a copy, imitation, reproduction, fake version of what God has in store for them. They are not willing to come up with the resource so instead they invest in a copy of the real thing. And just like I proudly walked around with my fake Louis Vuitton hanging off my arm, many people are proudly carrying around such poor versions of the real thing. The enemy is smiling in sadistic pride to see you so fooled and blinded.

It is only when you are faced with someone who is carrying a real and authentic outworking of God, that what you are holding all of a sudden seems so far less than perfect. In fact, it seems totally inadequate and even embarrassing. Aspects you had never noticed before now seem glaringly imperfect in the light of God. Nothing can stand up against what comes from God's own hand. Nothing can even come close. Every good and perfect thing comes from His hand. So when it truly originated from God, it is stunningly perfect. Nothing of this world can even come close.

The Holy Spirit came into this world on the day of Pentecost, like tongues of fire above every believer's head in the upper room and the sound of rushing wind. When you are carrying an imitation calling, destiny, commission, promise land, it will seem fine until the presence of the Holy Spirit comes. When the Holy Spirit enters, He will refine what is in your hands by the fire, and the wind will blow the rubbish away. You will be left realizing that what you hold is worthless, and will want to put it down once and for all.

When the Holy Spirit comes upon you, he will illuminate what you really have. He will reveal if you have been tricked into believing this could be the real thing. It is not! We need to have spirit eyes to see what He needs us to see. You need to have the scales removed from your eyes to see what it is God sees. If you ask God to shine His light on what's hanging off your arm now, He will draw your attention to the small details to reveal if it is of a counterfeit nature or not. Just like one hundred dollar notes are held up to the light to prove their legitimacy, we need to hold up to the light of God what we have sold out to, to prove it's legitimacy.

THE TRUTH WILL SET YOU FREE

Jesus is the ultimate illuminator. He is the light of the world. Everywhere he went during his ministry, as we read in the Gospels, he revealed and illuminated what was really happening, what was really going on beneath the surface. He would see right through people and the facades they hid behind, and spoke directly to the main issue. He would bring to light that which others could not see. Through scripture we see him bending down, drawing in the dirt and asking for the person without sin to cast the first stone. We see him stopping and turning in the crowd of people to acknowledge and publicly speak out the healing that had just taken place for the woman with the issue of blood. We see him talking with the Samaritan woman at the well. We see him kissing Judas in acknowledgment of his ultimate betrayal. Jesus is the filter that the truth will be seen through.

When Jesus is our way, when he is our everything, we will see what we carry through him. He will illuminate the truth to us and reveal what God has created, the ultimate designer, and what has been replicated and far less than perfect. Often when we are going through life carrying those things that feel less than perfect, and we see someone else who has got the real deal, we can easily become resentful and jealous of the other person. Our hurt, anger, and frustration is quickly misguided against others who have done nothing wrong except for trust God with their lives completely and take what He is offering to them with the resource they have acquired. We should not be envious, jealous, or angry with these people. We should do everything we can to come alongside them in whatever capacity is possible, and learn from them how they do life. God created us to live in community with one another. Although He is the most important relationship we have in our lives, God doesn't want us to become reliant only on Him. He wants us to look to each other and lean on one another and learn from each other. God said to love Him, and to also love each other. Loving someone does not include being spiteful, malicious, or hurtful. Women are the masters of being mean and knowing just how to make someone feel terrible. Because we are so in tune with emotions, we are skilled at using emotions to cause pain.

We must never forget that we are not fighting flesh and blood. But instead we are fighting principalities and rulers of the spiritual realm. Make sure you remain focused on who you are fighting. The most casualties in any war are the casualties resulting from friendly fire. We are on the same team ladies. We are in this together. It is foolish to fight against those you admire so much. When Jesus is in his rightful position in your life and is revealing the truth, you will see and understand that these other people who are carrying some pretty spectacular stuff are not the enemy. Be brave enough to celebrate them, and praise them, and come alongside them. It may be someone you have never met, but just look at from a distance. Don't be critical of all they are receiving and carrying. Pray for them, support them in whatever way you can. Let the people within your world hear your cheers, not your criticisms or silence.

Stuart and I have always had people in our life who just don't get us. To be truthful, it doesn't really affect us that much. We understand there will always be people who don't like what you are doing. Everywhere Jesus went, he was mocked, scorned and treated badly. For the most part we can shrug our shoulders and move on, although there have been situations which have been hurtful. I don't even begin to understand, except that when you take a hold of the Prada God has for you, it can have all sorts of affects on those around you. Surely we should all know God has a Heaven filled with Prada and instead of being resentful of what someone else has, we should be using our energies to go after our own.

I have been in churches before that feel just like a fake handbag. On the surface, they appear to be the real deal. But when you know the authentic version well, you know what details to look for to prove authenticity. Color, design, zips, logos, lining—any of these aspects can easily reveal the counterfeit nature of a handbag. Tithing, worship, welcome, how children are treated—any of these aspects can reveal the counterfeit nature of a church.

DO NOT FAKE IT UNTIL YOU MAKE IT

It is better to not have any designer handbag, than to carry a fake. There is a cheap and nasty feel to counterfeit handbags. There is nothing cheap or nasty about God. If we are representing Jesus, re-presenting him, we cannot poison his image with cheap and nasty. There are nannies who are given designer diaper bags to carry with them so as to keep the reputation of the family they are working for intact. The mother of the child does not want their child to be seen with a nanny that is carrying a cheap and nasty bag. They give them the bag to carry, to ensure they are equipped with the best. Thus is their passion for protecting their family's name. How much more should we be doing to protect the name of Jesus? If we are about our Father's business, and profess to the world we are God's sons and daughters, how important is it that we protect His reputation and carry only the very best, rather than cheap and nasty.

Once you have had the pleasure and privilege of owning a legitimate, authentic designer handbag, you will never go back to owning a fake. You just can't do it! Since my fake Louis Vuitton purchase in Fiji, I have been spoiled with not one but three designer handbags. Stuart has made the trip down Fifth Avenue, and made three purchases in as many years, for my birthday gifts. My first-ever designer handbag was classic, tan, calf leather Prada. The second was a cream and grey Louis Vuitton. The third was patent, black leather Louis Vuitton. I love all these bags, and love to carry any one of them with me wherever I may be going. I know these bags well. I have an intimate knowledge of their look, smell, and feel. I can easily spot another handbag like mine on the street and just as easily spot a fake version of mine. The discernment I have now that I am the owner of these bags is phenomenal.

Once you have experienced the real and authentic promises, mandates, and experiences of God, you will be ruined in the best possible way. You will never be able to go back to making do with cheap imitations. You will carry what God has given you with such excitement and wonder that you will be unable to carry anything short of this again. You will also gain such a level of discernment that you will immediately be able to tell what is the work and hand of God and what is not.

Stuart and I were invited to attend the Bethel Leadership Advance Conference within the first couple of months of our arrival in New York City. We had heard so much about Bethel and couldn't wait to experience the power of God in this church for ourselves. After three days of worshipping, listening to the word, receiving prayer and prophecy, and making connections and friends, we were forever changed. We have never experienced church in the way we experienced it at Bethel, and it left us in a state of never, ever wanting to go back to anything less again.

It says in the Psalms to "taste and see how good God is." Once you have tasted of what He has for you, you will do everything you can to never go back to anything less again. It is our hunger and thirst for Him that will place us in the exact position He needs us to be, so we can build the resource to make those things we have a taste for, our reality.

One of the foundational visions of The Salvation Army NYC is that this church would see the supernatural become the normal. When New Yorkers get a taste of the supernatural and see the evidence of the outworkings of this truth in their lives, they will never want to go back to operating within the limitations of the natural. Therefore, they will do whatever it takes to have this supernatural breakthrough and power at work in their lives every day. We won't have to set out to try and convince people to buy into the vision of the church, they will be compelled to be part of it because of the desire in their spirits for more of what they have tasted.

YOU GET WHAT YOU PAY FOR

A fundamental difference between an original designer handbag, and a replica or fake version, is the overall quality of the handbag itself. If the first principle of shopping is, "If you have to ask the price, you probably can't afford it," then the second principle is "You get what you pay for." When you are paying a fraction of the price for a fake handbag as you would for the real thing, you will get a fraction of the quality as well. Again, it wasn't until I owned an expensive handbag that I noticed the magnificence of quality. From the first sight, touch, smell of the designer handbag, you know that you have something special in your hands. It is different from anything else you have ever held. In fact, no other handbag can even come close.

You may be thinking, "Seriously, a handbag is a handbag!" How wrong this statement is.

One thing I noticed about my first Prada handbag was the softness of the leather. My fake version was extremely stiff in it's leather exterior. There was a remarkable difference in the way the handbag felt when handling it.

From the moment you pick up what God has for you, you will notice a remarkable difference from anything else you have ever carried. There will be ease and softness to the Prada of God. Replica, cheap versions of His plans are much stiffer, harder to handle, more awkward and set. There is not the same natural feel. You are not compelled to keep touching, keeping a personal involvement on what is happening when the environment seems hard and uninviting. But when there is softness, we will want to keep reaching out and having a physical closeness to everything that is happening in Jesus' name. We won't be able to keep our hands off! It won't be an elusive, distant, cold, hard gospel, but rather a warm, loving, approachable, tender, soft expression of God's heart in this world.

The leather on an authentic designer handbag continues to get better with age. There is something about the natural lifespan of this leather that continues to bring out a new level of beauty as the years go by. The leather becomes even softer with age, and a whole new range of beautiful color tones come to the forefront.

So too, there is a natural beauty that can be evidenced by a long-standing work of God. There is richness in its heritage and a beauty that cannot be bought. It is an organic process that happens over time, and each angle reveals another layer and level of God's work.

This is not the case with a copy version of a designer handbag. The leather on these things gets harder over time, cracking, collecting dirt, and looking worse for the wear. The bag loses its initial look, and is left looking shabby and un-kept.

When we try and replace the things God has for us with the cheaper option, it will not last the test of time. It may look great for a season. It may be hard to tell the difference between the copy and the real deal for a while. But as time goes on, cracks will appear. There is only so long that ministries can operate without a real and authentic touch of Heaven. Man-made will go so far, but it will inevitably come to an end. Instead of a beauty that deepens and starts to shine out and take on a whole new level of influence, the beauty of a replica will lessen and dull and fade away into oblivion. People will move onto the next new thing, and you will be left holding a has-been, burnt out, outdated, had it's hey day kinda deal. Like a city that feels old and dingy and decrepit, and yet you sense it was once a thriving place to be, you will be standing in the ghost town of a once alive ministry, wondering what happened, what went wrong.

Nothing went wrong. It was always going to be this way. It had to be, because it was never the design from God's hands. It was the man-made version. A fake designer handbag can never grow up to be a real designer handbag. That's not how it works. It's either a designer handbag or it's not. No amount of wishing or praying or fasting or giving can change its identity. You can change. Your resource can change. You can put one down and take up the other. But you can't turn a fake into the real thing. You're not the fairy godmother. And even if you were, the clock is always going to strike midnight. Everything will go back to how it always was.

A lot of churches and ministries and expressions of God start out strong. There is a passion and a desire and a bank of good ideas and it's all systems go for a while. People start coming alongside what is happening, progress is made, fruit is seen. And then… and then you start getting tired. Mistakes get made. People get hurt.

Everything seems hard. Limitations cannot be overcome. Effectiveness plateaus. People alongside start to distance themselves. Support starts to wane. There is disunity. The heart of the work starts to crumble. You have enough, and decide to call it a day. There is no beauty in this. There is no richness of hidden beauty that comes out over time.

When God creates something, it just keeps getting better and better. It is surely one of the most telling signs that something is from God. I know my marriage is from God's own hand. I thought I could not possibly love Stuart any more than I did on the day I became his bride. And yet, eighteen years later, I love him so much more than I did back then. The love we share continues to grow everyday. Does that mean that we have not had hard days, or times when marriage has been difficult? Absolutely not! We have had our share of heartaches and struggles, but because God created our marriage, there is a depth and beauty within it, that in an instant can be brought to life once again. You can't do that with something the world has created. When the shine has gone, it's gone!

WHAT'S IN YOUR HAND?

This is why it is so important that you are able to discern exactly what it is you have in your hand. You could be holding a God-designed masterpiece in your hands, but it has gotten a little dusty and beaten up and isn't looking too good. The truth is, the identity is still the same, and the purpose and power and beauty are still the same. In an instant, God can take the ruins of what has become of what He created and turn them into beauty once again. That is the power of what God designs. So often we go through life never fully understanding what it is we have in our hands.

In saying all of this, it still can be tricky for most people to tell a fake from the real thing just by seeing the outside of a handbag. Some of these manufacturers are clever at imitating what they have seen created in the design houses. So often it is the inside of the handbag where the biggest differences lie. The lining on a designer handbag is as exquisite as any of the outside detail. There is usually a silk lining with the name of the designer printed all over it. There can also be a seal or badge of the designer inside as well. This adds another level of authenticity to the handbag and marks the inside with the designer's identity.

I love the thought of this image. From the outside, we can appear to be the same as other people around us. It can appear that we are carrying the same types of things in our hands and going about the same type of business, until people see what is on the inside. On the inside of every Christian is the seal and identity of Jesus who purchased our life with his blood. The lining of our souls is exquisite, and his beauty is within us. When we are holding what He has given to us, when we are carrying the very thing that He has made available to us through the resource of our faith and willingness to give Him full control, from the inside out we will be marked by Him. From the very core of what we are holding, you will be able to see the mark of God. There will be no mistake in distinguishing where this has originated from and whom this belongs to. Because at the heart of it all, we can carry it, but it always belongs to God.

No matter how hard manufacturers may try, no matter how much effort is given, no matter how much money is thrown at it, there are just some things that cannot be reproduced. So close, and yet so far away. In it's essence, a fake designer handbag could not be further away from the original it aims to be.

No matter how hard the enemy tries to manufacture and imitate what God can do, there are just some things that cannot be reproduced. God is a God of miracles, signs, and wonders, and the reality of these cannot be copied.

After that initial New Year's Eve, when Stuart and I gave breath to the God whispers we had both heard, we started to experience signs and wonders like never before in our lives. God was so completely in this, and He was showing us signs that all pointed to Him. When times of doubt would invade our thoughts and minds, we would remember the signs God had shown us, the wonders we had experienced, and our faith was strengthened as we saw again and believed He was at work in our life. It was not something man-made or offered from the world.

From the outset we saw His hand when we both spoke of the same thing that God had been telling us separately. That was the first of many confirmations and signs. Then, I had an experience in the middle of one night, when we were all soundly asleep. I stirred in my sleep, and slightly opened my eyes, as I was in that half-awake, half-asleep zone. Just as I was about to try and fall back to sleep, out of nowhere I felt this incredible pressure on top of me. I was laying flat on my back, and it felt like someone was sitting on my chest. My whole body was being pressed into the mattress. Stuart was asleep right beside me, but I couldn't move a muscle to reach out to him. I couldn't make any sound. I just lay there in a frozen state. As I was being pressed into the bed, I saw a beam of light coming from inside my mouth and reaching upward toward the ceiling. There were small glittering specks all through the beam of light. I was so scared. My initial thought was that I was dying. That my spirit was being taken away from my body and I was about to die. In that moment, all I could do was to say silently to God, "I love you, I love you, I love you, I love you, I love you." I repeated this over and over until the light disappeared and the sensation stopped. By this time I was wide-awake. My heart was beating furiously. As I lay there in the aftermath, I started to immediately doubt what I had just experienced. Was it just a weird dream? As soon as I thought this, boom, my body was being squashed again! Except this time, I didn't think I was dying. I thought that instead of taking something away from me, God was connecting me to Himself in a new way. Again, the presence of what was happening left as quickly as it had begun.

I lay there in the dark of our bedroom that night, knowing that something profound had just happened to me. God was on me and in me for a new season, for a new assignment, for a new commission. I felt empowered, excited, and energized. I had no idea of what had just happened, but I knew it was God, and I knew it was for me.

It was six months later that Stuart was reading a book by Bill Johnson in bed one night. Suddenly, he thrust the book into my face and asked me to read the passage he was pointing to. As I read the page, I read of Bill Johnson's experience one night that was so similar to what I had experienced. We still didn't really understand what it all meant, but Stuart and I were both so excited to sense that God had revealed Himself to me in a very special way. We knew God was with us in unprecedented levels, and we were hungering and thirsting for Him more than ever before.

This couldn't be made up. This couldn't be manufactured. This was a sign from God to reveal His plans and purposes for us were bigger than we had ever experienced before. We were encouraged to keep going, to press in further. We felt equipped with more of Him in us. So many times I have thought about my experience that night. So many times when I worry that I have made all of this up in my own head and it isn't even what God planned for us, I then think about the experience that night. That was real. I know it. I felt it. I lived it. That was as real to me as the book or electronic device you are reading this from. God gave me the certainty of that experience to reinforce the certainty of His words and plans over our lives. God knew I would need that experience, and He gave it to me to prove His authenticity and to distinguish this from being anything else.

Since then Stuart and I have experienced gold dust on our hands after we had worshipped and prayed, gold dust all over the front of our clothes, gold dust all over the tablecloth of the table where we were sitting sharing with our dear friends about all God was doing. So many times when we would pray or share or worship God, with New York in our hearts, He would reveal signs and wonders that would continually point us to Him and confirm and reveal His plans and identity in it all.

5

THE LAND OF THE BOUTIQUE

"Enter through the narrow gate. For wide is the gate and broad is the road that leads to destruction, and many enter through it. But small is the gate and narrow the road that leads to life, and only a few find it." Matthew 7:13-14 (NIV)

Any serious shopper would know there are shops and then there are boutiques. Shops are big, open, busy, easy, and filled to the brim with merchandise. Boutiques are small, intimate, quiet, personal, and show limited pieces at any one time. There is nothing mass-market about boutiques and they sit on a level all their own.

God works in boutiques. The things God has for your life will only be found in a boutique environment. In saying this, we know God's ways are different from our ways, and His thoughts are higher than our thoughts, and this principle is again true in the boutique context. God's boutiques don't look like the kind we would imagine them to be. In fact, they could look so opposite to what we expect that we could easily disregard them and walk straight past.

God uses intimate environments, humble beginnings, small sizes, minimalist quantities, and yet the finest of details to showcase what He has for us to step into and take a hold of. There is a beauty about these spaces that is deep and profound, and the Prada God has for you will only ever be available in His boutique.

Designer handbags are sold in boutiques rather than stores. In the rare instance of a designer handbag being sold in a store, there will be a boutique-style fitting within the store that houses the designer handbags. Exclusive, bigger stores have a separate designated area where the designer handbags are given their own identity and framework. But mostly, it's the small boutique feel when you are in the market for a designer handbag.

THE MARK OF A BOUTIQUE

These boutiques are marked differently from any other stores. First, they have the most amazing window displays. There is not a lot of stock on display, but the way it has been designed is visually amazing. Often you will see people on Fifth Avenue stopping to take photos of the window displays. The windows are a work of art in themselves.

The night Bergdorf Goodman unveiled its holiday windows last year, Stuart and I headed down to Fifth Avenue to check them out. It was a freezing cold night, and yet it didn't deter us or anyone else who was there. People were lining the sidewalk looking and taking photos of the new displays. And it was worth every goose bump and shiver! The windows were stunning. There has been a documentary made about these windows, and there is a team of people whose job it is to plan these displays and make them a reality. Amazing!

The next aspect of the boutique is the doorkeeper. There is a man standing near the double front doors of these boutiques who is ready to open the door for you. He greets you with a smile, a nod of the head, and a friendly welcoming sentence. You are immediately put at ease and he helps you to feel like you not only belong in a place like this, but you are so welcome in this place.

Then there are the sales assistants, who are standing behind the counters with a smile on their faces. They are impeccably dressed, with their hair and make-up done beautifully. They too welcome you with a smile and a greeting, and offer to assist you. I have even come across sales assistants in these boutiques that offer me something to drink: water, champagne, anything that took my fancy. Their aim is to help you enjoy your experience so you walk back out of that boutique holding something new in your hands.

And of course, our gaze then shifts to the shelves and cabinets, as we look over the handbags on display. Every bag our eye can see is as beautiful as the next. There are not ten handbags of the same style all sitting on the shelf together; there is only one of each design and style. It isn't a "help yourself to one off the shelf" type of situation, it is more a "indicate which one you like and the assistant will bring it to you," type of situation.

Again, the prices are nowhere to be seen at this point. The sales assistant will not even talk price with you unless you specifically ask. The small envelope hidden within the handbag just adds to the beauty and drama of this whole experience. It all feels so glamorous!

Because there are not crowds of people in these boutiques, the ratio of sales assistants to customers is quite high. This translates into a sales assistant who is more than happy to bring you as many handbags as you would like to see. There is no pressure to make a quick decision; you can take as long as you want, savoring every moment of this process.

When you are blessed to be able to purchase one of these handbags, you do not receive the handbag that has been sitting on the shelf. The sales assistant will disappear, and then bring you out a brand new handbag that looks as though it has come straight out of the designer's hands. The quality is impeccable, and it shines like a precious diamond. You are asked to have a look at this particular handbag, and approve this as your purchase.

Once you have given the final acceptance of the handbag you wish to purchase, and the resource has been received and accepted, the handbag is then packaged. The handbag is placed inside a cloth bag as a protective layer. Then the handbag, within the cloth bag, is placed inside a beautiful box. The box is then decorated with a ribbon tied around the package with a beautiful bow on top. Finally, the box is placed in a shiny paper bag, with the designer's label and name printed on the front.

As you take hold of the bag, with your brand new purchase safely inside, there is a genuine feeling of excitement for you, from the whole host of sales assistants that line the sides of the boutique. You walk out of that place feeling like you are on top of the world. What an amazing feeling!

THE BOUTIQUE OF CHURCH

This experience should be what church feels like for whoever decides to step in from the street. From the moment you come across a house of God, you should be immediately captivated by the display you can see from outside the doors. It's not just about what is going on inside the four walls of a church, it's about what the world can see looking from the outside in. It should stop them in their tracks! It should be so beautiful they will want to try and capture what they see somehow. And it should give them the motivation to move beyond the sidewalk to inside the front doors.

No matter how many hours you spend window-shopping, you will never walk away with a purchase from merely looking through the glass to what is on the other side. Sure, window-shopping is safe; you don't have to put yourself out there to be a window shopper. You don't have to step into an environment that may feel foreign and daunting and a little unnerving, not knowing what to expect. But without that element of risk, you have no opportunity to make a purchase.

You will never take hold of all God has for you if all you ever do is window-shop your way through life. God doesn't need more window shoppers. Nothing is achieved in your life if all you ever do is gaze upon a sample of what could be yours. Sure, window-shopping can be a great motivator and a beautiful example of the types of things God has designed for you. But we need to move beyond this stage. We are coming into a time in history where the windows of Heaven are displayed more magnificently than ever before through the church. Churches all across the world are rising up to take their places as the most exquisite, breathtaking, stunning boutiques showcasing the very best of Heaven.

God wants His church to be a place where people are unable to walk past without noticing what is happening, and to be in awe of the beauty that is radiating from that place. God wants us to not only acknowledge the beauty and the wonder of the church from afar, but to step inside the very heart of the church and take all that He has in stock for us to take.

What God has for you can only be received through the church, the ultimate boutique of Heaven. Here is a place that houses the works of God so beautifully; it is a place to behold. And this place is for the whosoever. Jesus didn't come to this earth and die for a select group of people. He came for everyone. He loves everyone. I smile to myself when people ask us which demographic our church focuses on. "Who are you aiming at?" Our reply is always the same. We're aiming for the people God loves, the people Jesus gave his life for, everyone we can see, the whosoever.

The months following Stuart and my New Year's Eve talk on the hammock was an exhilarating yet nerve-wracking time. We were out on the pavement, and felt like we had just seen the most amazing boutique filled with magnificence beyond our wildest dreams. We launched ourselves into the word, and committed much of our days to leaving room for God to move in us.

One morning during this period of time, I was walking on the treadmill in the garage of our home. I had felt an urging from God to take care of my physical body, to ensure that I was physically fit and healthy so as to be able to undertake everything He had for me to do. I had never really done any exercise in life up until this point. I was blessed with a fast metabolism, and could keep reasonably thin by just having good genetics. Crazy favored, I know. Anyway, I had come into a space where I knew I needed to take God at His word in every aspect of life, so I found myself waking up at 5:15am every morning to get a good forty-five minute walk in before the day began.

Walking on a treadmill can be excruciatingly boring, especially when you're facing the back of your garage wall. I needed something to do other than watch the timer slowly creep up, second by second. I tried to read my bible. Let's just say that didn't work out too well. Lucky I had clipped the emergency safety latch to the bottom of my shirt! I tried listening to music, but couldn't stop myself from joining in, singing in full voice, much to the annoyance of my family who was still sleeping. I then discovered podcasts. Hallelujah! Now I could be walking and also keep my mind active and productive, which at that time was important to me. I struggled to think of myself ever wasting time.

One such morning, I was walking and listening to a Jentezen Franklin podcast, one of my all time favorite preachers. He was talking about right people, right place, right plan. Out of nowhere, I felt this urgency that we had to go to New York. I could feel God's promptings encouraging me that if we went to New York, He would be able to reveal more to us. As soon as I acknowledged what He was saying to me, it all seemed to make perfect sense.

I met Stuart that morning for breakfast at a cafe near our office. I told him I didn't know how this would work logistically, but I really felt that God needed us to go to New York as soon as possible. I knew more would be revealed to us then. Stuart was completely shocked, and his mind immediately went into overdrive at the thought of trying to make this work. It was a busy time in our business, cash reserves were not high, and it would be a mammoth exercise to get the four of us to New York from Australia. But, as we were about to discover, when God calls you to do something, He makes the way where it seems there is no way. A few short months later, we were sitting on a Delta plane about to leave for our first ever trip to New York City. Stuart had worked so hard to get us to this point. I could see the wave of relief wash over his face when we all took our seats and buckled our seat belts.

Being rookie travelers at this point, we opted for window seats rather than aisle seats. This meant that between me and the aisle, sat a large American football player, whose body took up a huge amount of space. We talked for a little while, and then he fell fast asleep. The Sydney to LA flight is an enormous stretch of time, so I was trapped for the next fourteen hours. I was feeling too guilty about trying to get past this man so I could go to the bathroom. So I figured that I would just stop drinking, so that I wouldn't have to disturb him. Good in theory. As we were landing in LA, I didn't feel very well. In fact, as I went to stand up, I felt like I was going to faint and vomit at the same time.

I dragged myself off the plane and started to proceed through LA customs. I was really struggling. We were the very last in line in customs, and I was lying on the ground, a grey kind of color. I was dehydrated and having massive sugar lows. Stuart had the two children, eight suitcases, four pieces of hand luggage, and me on the ground. He leaned down and in his most loving, stern voice, told me to GET UP or else they wouldn't let me on the next flight. Another flight? I groaned at the thought. Somehow I managed to get it together enough to go through customs, drop off our luggage, and get to our departure gate for the LA to JFK flight. Praise Jesus!

Before too long, we were landing in JFK, and the nightmares of the flight quickly dissipated. We were in New York City! As we loaded our luggage into a car, and headed towards an apartment I had organized in Manhattan, an excitement started to build within me. It was quite late at night, and the lights of the city were on for all to see. As we approached Manhattan, I looked out of the window of the car and caught that first glimpse of the iconic New York City skyline. My heart leapt out of my chest. It was love at first sight. In a moment, I was changed forever. I cannot describe it, apart from the fact that there was something about this city that had completely stolen my heart. I was never going to be the same again. I sat there in the car, tears streaming down my face. I knew why God needed us to be here on this trip. He needed us to love this place, because He knew that love is the greatest motivator of all. Everything about us in New York City, had to come from a place, platform and framework of love. Without love, none of what He had for us would be possible. Love was the key to all of this.

We left New York after two and a half weeks. To be truthful, we left with even more questions than when we arrived. But one thing was certain: New York City had a piece of us. God had revealed this place to be our promised land, and we knew somehow, someway, our destiny was tied to this place. We had tried to explore a few options, in what made sense to us, only to come across closed doors. We didn't really know what was happening, but we knew the One that did. That was enough for now.

It was another sixteen months before we would be back in New York City. Like the Israelites in the wilderness, God had been giving us fresh manna every day during this time. We were learning many lessons from Him and being prepared in ways we didn't even realize. It was the hardest period we had ever experienced. It brought us to a level of reliance on God that we had never experienced before. In hindsight, it was all part of His perfect plan.

Preparing to return to New York City, this time for just over four weeks, we were certain God would have more for us to know and understand. Our imaginations were running wild at this point, trying to imagine just what it was God had for us in this city. One night as I slept, God gave me a profound dream. I dreamt that Stuart and I were in a small hall with rows of chairs, and a center aisle. The majority of the people sitting in the chairs were wearing Salvation Army uniforms, so I knew in an instant that I was in a Salvation Army church meeting. I was standing at the front, preaching a giving message in preparation for the offering to be taken up. At the back corner of the hall was a doorway. The door had half opened, and as I saw through, I caught a glimpse of an enormous auditorium filled with people standing around talking and laughing, in a pre-service kind of vibe. None of these people were wearing Salvation Army uniforms. Just as I had seen through the door, someone from The Salvation Army walked up and closed it. I kept speaking from the front but now started to motion to Stuart with my eyes and head wobbles, for him to go over and open the door again. How desperately I wanted to be able to go from this small hall into the large auditorium. I wanted to be in that type of service rather than the one I found myself in. I kept thinking to myself, if there were ever any chance of getting in there, this door would have to stay open so the way could be made.

Every time Stuart would go and try and open the door, someone from The Salvation Army would close it.

I woke up from this dream, knowing that God had given me a message. I needed to search His heart and make sure I heard what He was saying to me. As I prayed and waited before God in prayer, I turned to my Bible and read from John 10. In this particular passage, it was talking about the sheep and the gate. Verses 1-5, 6 read, "I assure you, anyone who sneaks over the wall of a sheepfold, rather than going through the gate, must surely be a thief and a robber! For a shepherd enters through the gate. The gatekeeper opens the gate for him, and the sheep hear his voice and come to him. He calls his own sheep by name and leads them out. After he has gathered his own flock, he walks ahead of them, and they follow him because they recognize his voice. They won't follow a stranger; they will run from him because they don't recognize his voice," Jesus explained to them, "I assure you, I am the gate for the sheep."

In that moment I felt the stabbing emphasis of God in my heart. "They follow him because they recognize his voice. They won't follow a stranger." Instantly I knew that whatever God had planned for us in New York City, it was going to be framed within The Salvation Army. God had given me that dream, and He had given me the explanation. He was the gate! He was that doorway in my dream. The only way to get into the big auditorium was to enter into the small boutique hall and go through Jesus into the big arena. There were no shortcuts here, no trying to sneak over the gate. We had to do it the way God had planned. And because we were Salvationists, God was going to use us to speak to them and lead them out. They would follow us because we were one of them;

they were never going to follow a stranger.

Again, I needed to get my courage to go and share this with Stuart. Although I had grown up in The Salvation Army since I gave my heart to Jesus at age seven, and Stuart had given his heart to Jesus in a Salvation Army Good Friday service in 1993, we were not your typical Salvationists. In fact, we were very different to the traditional Salvation Army mold. We didn't connect with the more formal expressions of The Salvation Army church, and instead had been part of a leadership team that had planted and grown a new expression of The Salvation Army in Newcastle, Australia. So I was nervous to approach this subject with Stuart. Yet again, God had already gone before me. As I spoke about the dream and the meaning of this image, Stuart's expression remained blank. Once I had finished, he told me that he knew this conversation was coming. In fact, he had known for quite some time the exact message that God had given to me. Stuart was waiting for God to give me the message, to confirm it in his heart that he had heard correctly.

Our heads were spinning at this stage. At no time on our first visit to New York City did we even think to attend or look at The Salvation Army over there. It just didn't even come up in our thinking. This was so clearly from God, and not a scheme we had thought up or imagined. It just so happened, a nice little God-incidence, I was speaking at a Salvation Army combined meeting about prayer that week. I went to that meeting with a heightened sensation of what it was God needed me to do, say, see. I was so open to Him.

The meeting was a collection of people from Salvation Armies all over our area. Each representative would stand and talk about what was happening in their church. It was a hot November morning in Australia, and here we were sitting around a non-air conditioned hall, in full Salvation Army uniform, brass band playing, trying to focus on the days ahead, but continually listening to people who kept slipping back into reminiscing about the days gone by. I felt so out of touch with the world going on around us. I felt sadness in my spirit. I wanted to stand up and scream, "No! It's not supposed to be this way! This wasn't the vision William and Catherine Booth birthed!"

I went home that day with such an unsettled feeling in my heart. I couldn't imagine what it was God was up to. I felt such a passion for The Salvation Army, yet at the same time, such sadness. As I sat later, trying to sort through everything that was racing through my head, I felt God tell me to send an email to the leader of the entire Territory who was present in the meeting that day. Commissioner James Condon is a mighty man of God whom we love, admire, and look up to. I penned an email to him, being very honest with the way I was feeling. I expressed my love for The Salvation Army, as well as my sadness the meeting had evoked the other day. I told him we were heading to New York, and we were going to seek out The Salvation Army there. I shared that God had awakened our hearts to the wider Salvation Army, and we were so keen to find out why.

A matter of weeks later, we arrived for the second time in New York City. As soon as we landed, it felt like I was arriving home. It was such an unusual feeling. We arrived on a Friday night, and first thing Saturday we found a Salvation Army bell ringer in Times Square to ask where the churches of The Salvation Army were in this area. The man told us two different churches, one in the Times Square area, and one down on 14th Street. The next morning we overslept and missed the first service at the Times Square Salvation Army, which was close to where we were staying. Instead, we jumped in a cab and headed to 14th Street. As we hopped out of the cab, we stood on the sidewalk in front of a huge church building. There were big golden iron gates across the front of the building, and as we tried to open them, we realized they were locked. Stuart, myself, Madeline, and Gabriel were all trying to open these gates. We thought they must lock out any latecomers! As we stood there not knowing what to do, a gentleman who was working on the building yelled out to us and asked us what we were doing. We told him we wanted to go to church. He pointed down the sidewalk a bit further, and told us the church was down there. We looked down the sidewalk and saw a small sandwich board sign advertising a church service. We all hurried down the sidewalk and raced through the small doors.

As we entered the church we stood still and looked around. What we saw in that moment took my breath away. Here we found ourselves standing in a small hall, with rows of chairs set up. There were about thirty people present, with the majority in Salvation Army uniform. Attached to this hall stood a massive auditorium that seats fourteen hundred people. Stuart and I looked at one another. We both knew without having to say a word that this was the dream God had given to me. In that moment, as we sat down in that service, I heard God's voice tell me, "I want you to lead my people from here, to there." In an instant I knew. God's plans had been revealed. He had called us to New York City for this very reason and purpose. This was the mission ground. This was our destiny. This is where we would see God move in ways we could never even dream about.

As I tried to gain my composure, I started to look around the space where we were sitting. Here we were in the heart of New York City, the most amazing, alive, influential city in the world, and yet there were thirty people who gathered as The Salvation Army. There was a massive arena sitting empty next door. How had this happened? What had happened to the vision that was obviously here when that huge auditorium was built? Again God spoke, interjecting into my thoughts. He spoke about the Parable of the Wedding Feast. He told me the invited guests had not come, and it was time to go out to the highways and the byways, and fill His house. He didn't ask us to minister to a certain demographic of people. He didn't tell us to gather a designated group together. He told us, "Now go out to the street corners and invite everyone you see." (Matthew 22:9) I cried throughout the entire service.

THE HUMILITY OF GOD'S BOUTIQUE

There are so many layers to the way God worked in this situation, so many facets to this story. I see the boutique in its significance and relevance here. Here I see the boutique as the small, intimate, foreign, unusual place, which serves as the entry point for taking hold of all that God has for you. And I also see the boutique as a picture of the church. The narrow road entry point into a life that is so big, and full, and expansive.

God is all about love, and He is all about humility. Jesus entered the world through the boutique of not only a baby, but a baby born in a barnyard. Jesus entered Jerusalem on Palm Sunday through the boutique of a donkey. Over and over again in the scriptures we read stories of men and women who God was raising up to do extraordinary works in His name, who had to go through the boutique before they could step into the arena. Abraham, Moses, David, Esther, Joseph, all had to enter into the boutique, the small, the intimate, the purposed environment and entry point to the days ahead. God orchestrated for us to enter New York City through the boutique of a small Salvation Army Corps. With everything that I am, I praise God for leading me to that place.

You could be in the boutique right now, and yet you are discounting it's worth and value. Don't despise small beginnings. Small, humble, unusual, or out of the ordinary is not bad. You cannot sneak into what God has for you. No matter how hard you try, it just will not work. You will become discouraged and exhausted by continually trying to open gates that are locked and doors that keep being closed again. If you are continually trying to enter into your promise land in the same way, and yet always coming up against the same blocks, then that is not God's entry point for you. As hard as it may be, as much time as you think you are wasting, as confusing as it all can seem, when the gates and doors and windows of opportunity are not opening before you, stand back, be still before God and go wherever He leads you to go.

You may be walking down the sidewalk into a foreign place, an environment that looks nothing like the dreams in your heart. Trust Him! The manger in a barnyard looks nothing like the throne of a King, and it was the way God chose for Jesus to enter this world and accomplish all that was in his destiny to accomplish. Where

God leads you may not look anything like where you want to be, but it may be just the way God has chosen for you to enter into all that He has for you to do and accomplish. Will you be humble enough to accept His way and lower yourself to come into what He has? Or will your pride be so immovable you discount yourself before you have ever had the opportunity to start?

If Stuart and I had of walked into that small hall that Sunday morning in December and turned up our nose and thought, "no way," we never would be living in New York City now, building His church in the arena He has given to us. If we had not been willing to lower ourselves, and leave the comforts and luxuries we had, and empty ourselves of any of our own desires and ambitions, we would not have received the full portion of His anointing over our lives to go about His business on the streets of New York City through The Salvation Army.

You will never see the full extent of where God is leading you until you are brave enough to step inside. When you first walk through the doors of your boutique it may be like nothing you have ever experienced before. Life transformation will be yours when you follow the call of God, let Him direct your paths, and not just window shop but step over the threshold. This will not only set you in the market for a fine Prada piece, it will ensure that you have the resource to be able to claim it as your own. No longer will these promises be displayed as a wish list, imagine if, maybe one day. These promises will become yours to live, feel, love, and declare.

Jesus is the way. Jesus is the door. Our responsibility is to not only go where God is leading us, stepping into all that He has for us, taking a hold of everything that is stored up for us, we also have a responsibility to others. God commanded us to love Him, and then to also love others. As people who know and love Jesus, we become like the doorman at the front of the boutique. It is our role to be ready and waiting to open the door, making the way clear and welcoming the whosoever who wants to come into a relationship with Jesus and enter into his church.

The church is the ultimate boutique. It is an intimate environment we enter into and take hold of a Savior who unlocks our eternity.

Just as the boutiques have a doorman at the front, ready and waiting to welcome you in, we need to be standing at the doorposts of our churches, on the lookout, ready to welcome those who want to come in. There are no criteria, no expectations, no judgments to be made here. You need to smile, greet, comfort, and assure people who are out on the sidewalk that this door is the way to transformation in the best possible way.

I am always interested to see the ushers who stand at the entry point of a church. This is such a critical role. This person is the first contact a person will have with your church, which could be the only church they have ever experienced. The usher has the very real privilege, and yet responsibility, to usher people into the house of God. How important is it that this usher is smiling, and happy, and shining with the love of Jesus? How important is it to instantly make people feel a sense of peace that everything is going to be all right when they come through this door?

I have been in a church where the first usher we came across asked us for the first four weeks we attended if this was our first time at that church. At the four-week mark, I almost burst out laughing. I think I would have if it hadn't of been so sad. If this usher was saying this to us, then who else was he saying it to? I started to observe how others were greeted. Much to my horror, instead of being asked if this was their first time at church, other newcomers were asked if they were sure they were in the right place. The usher would tell them of another church that was meeting just a few doors up, and was making sure they didn't want to be there! Here we were praying that new people would not be able to walk past the church on the street, that something would compel them to come inside and see what was happening, and then the usher is asking them if they were really meant to come here! Oh my…

As the church, we are to line the shelves of Heaven and assist people to take hold of what God has for them. Our aim should be to see people leave the place where we have gathered as the church with something in their hands that they didn't have when they walked in. It could be a freedom from addiction, it could be a truth from the gospel, it could be a new friend to walk the hard days with, it could be a calling from God to do something they had never dreamed about, whatever it is, it will feel like a Prada handbag to the person who is carrying it out. There is nothing more exciting in life than being able to assist God, co-labor with Him, in order to outwork His plans and purposes in the lives of other people. There should be a tangible excitement every Sunday when you are watching people leave your church, equipped in ways they were not two hours before. It should break our heart to see people leaving empty handed.

There is such an excitement and momentum that will spread through your church when you are seeing person after person carrying the Prada God has for them. To think you have been able to play a small part in that will set your hearts alight. That is a church on fire. That is a breeding ground for the presence of God to come and for miracles to be witnessed. It is not ordinary to see people walking in with nothing, and then out with Prada. It just isn't! But that is exactly what we want to see happening in our church. We want a place where the supernatural is the natural, where the normal is the extraordinary, where there is such a presence and layer of God that amazing things happen to people just like you and me.

6

IT'S A STANDOUT

"You are the light of the world – like a city on a hilltop that cannot be hidden. No one lights a lamp and then puts it under a basket. Instead, a lamp is placed on a stand, where it gives light to everyone in the house." Matthew 5:14-15 (NLT)

One thing is certain about a designer handbag: it stands out in any crowd. In a sea of ordinary handbags, a designer bag will stand out every time. There is just something different about them. A Prada handbag is a beautiful thing.

How true is this when we think about the promises, callings, and inheritance of God over our lives. When we are walking in the promises of God, and holding onto all He has given to us, there is a beauty about us that stands out in the crowd. This is exactly how God wants it to be. He wants you to stand out because of the promises He has adorned your life with. He wants others to look at you and think, "I'll have what she's having." He wants you to be a light in this dark, often crazy world. He wants you to be different.

No one has a Prada handbag and tries to make it look like a Target handbag. Are you crazy?! Of course no one would do that. If you have a Prada handbag, you drape it over your arm and show it off for the world to see. How much more then should we be showing off all God has done in our lives. How much more should we be displaying all that His promises have brought into our lives? And yet, so often, people try and mask the work of God in themselves, and try to be ordinary. Are you crazy?! If you have the Prada of Heaven, you have what the world is so desperate to have. Don't try and hide it to fit in, show it off to lift Him up.

THE MARK OF THE DESIGNER

Designers are proud of their work and display their name and brand on every handbag they make. No matter if it is a Prada, Louis Vuitton, Chanel, or a host of other designer handbags, there will be an identifiable badge or label or icon on the handbag to identify who owns the design. God designed the promises and blessings and anointing you carry through life. They all originated from Him. His mark is therefore all over you. When people look at you, they will see the badge, icon, label of God on your life, and that is how we spread the good news of the Gospel.

Just before Jesus left this earth and ascended once again into Heaven, he gave the great commission. He instructed all of his disciples and followers to go and spread the good news of the gospel to the ends of the earth. These were his final instructions to us. How do we know if we are doing that? Well for starters, we have to make sure what we are spreading is in fact good news. If it isn't good news, then it isn't the Gospel!

There is nothing good about trying to fit into a world that you were never meant to fit into. Jesus said to be in the world, but not of it. The struggle of trying to appear normal and fit in when you just don't is not anybody's idea of a good time. This isn't good news. We need to learn and to teach others how to live in this world, carrying the blessings, favor, and promises of God over our lives, and how that gives us life in all it's fullness in this world and the next. Now that's good news.

New York City is a melting pot of humanity. If there is ever a place in this world where you can be who you really are, and not be worried about standing out or trying to fit in, it's on these streets. And yet, even on the streets of this amazing city, the favor of God makes you stand out among the masses. There is just something about the light in your eyes when you are going through your days with the love of God in your heart, and His truth in your mind. His promises and blessings frame everything you do.

We hadn't been in New York for long when I was on a crowded subway one afternoon. I had quickly learned that on subways you mind your business and stand quietly alongside your fellow travelers. I was sitting on a seat this day, my mind racing through a thousand different things, when the silence was broken by a booming man's voice yelling, "You're not from here are you?" I looked up to see who he was addressing, and I caught the intense stare of a man sitting opposite me, looking straight into my eyes. I must have looked startled, because he repeated the question, "You're not from here, are you?" I was conscious of every one else on the train now looking at me. I explained that I do live in New York City, but I have just moved from Australia. He smiled with a look of satisfaction of being right. "I knew it. You smile too much. New York women don't smile as much as you."

My heart sank. How sad this was. I could almost feel the sigh of Heaven as this sad truth was spoken out. Instead of feeling like I should be careful about smiling, and trying not to smile in order to fit in on these streets, I prayed in that moment and asked God to help me never lose my smile. If my smile is the mark of God on my life that I am carrying a measure of His love, mercy, and greatness, then let me never stop smiling! I make an effort now everywhere I go to smile at New Yorkers. It's not the normal, it's not the ordinary, but it's next level awesome. It sets you apart from the crowd and points to the designer whose workmanship you carry well.

THE PRADA PLATFORM

Carrying the Prada God gives to you puts you in spaces you never ever thought were possible. You don't stand out just for the sake of standing out; you are different because there is a purpose in your difference. God needs you to be different so He can show the world what they can have through Him. He needs you to relax and take hold of all you have received in His name, and show it off for the world to see. The greatest way to build faith is through testimony. When people around you are talking about amazing things that have happened in their lives through God, it makes your belief factor that it can happen to you get even stronger. The more stories of healing you hear, the more you believe you can be healed. The more stories of true love you hear, the more you believe you will find true love. Faith comes through hearing. So when you are speaking the language of Heaven, God will amplify your voice. God will set you apart. God will create a platform for you to showcase His work so all who see and hear you can believe.

It may be hard to imagine how someone like you could make an impact in the place where you are. The world seems so big and daunting sometimes. The noises of the world are so loud, its images so bright, its messages so in your face, but greater is He who lives in me than he who is in the world. No matter how loud the world can get, the roar of Heaven will pierce through it every single time. And it may not be in the big, out-there kind of way, it is often in the still small voice.

On our first visit to New York, God showed us many things about this city and gave us insight into how He works. There is a degree of influence you can hold in a small town like my hometown of Newcastle. You can walk through life shining all that God has given to you, and often be blessed to see the impact that has on others. But New York City is a whole different ballgame. I am just one, little, tiny, insignificant person in this great metropolis. Although I had completely and madly fallen in love with this city, I did feel totally insignificant and wondered how God would ever be able to use someone like me to make an impact on a city like this.

God showed me a very real example of His ability to make us known in the midst of the most public of places. It was a gorgeous Saturday morning, at the end of summer, in Central Park, New York City. If we are talking about a public space, it doesn't get a lot more public than this. There were people all through the park. The place was absolutely buzzing. There were joggers jogging, there were cyclists riding, there were families having picnics, there were roller skaters dancing to music, there were street performers playing their music, there were horses and carriages carrying tourists through the park, there were people getting married, there were people rowing boats, there were people taking photos, doing yoga, kids playing baseball, film shoots, modeling shoots, you name it, it was happening in the park this morning. Everywhere you looked, there were people enjoying this beautiful environment and what they were doing. Even celebrities could easily fit in here, just blending into the throng of people who were loving Central Park.

I had always wanted to ride through Central Park on a bike. It was one of those images I had in my mind of something that would be an amazing experience. I had seen so many people in the movies grab a bicycle and ride through the park, and it just looked magical. So being on an adventure with God already, trying to be daring and doing what was in our hearts to do, Stuart and I decided we would hire some bicycles and fulfill a desire we'd always had. We went to the closest hire place to investigate the bike situation. We quickly realized there were no children's bicycles available. Gabriel was 4-years-old, and Madeline was 8, and neither was strong enough to ride an adult bike. The man in the shop suggested we hire two tandem bicycles. That way, each child could have their own bike, but it would be attached to ours. Great! Fantastic! Wonderful idea, I thought.

It was quickly decided that Gabriel would go with me, and Madeline would be with Stuart. This seemed to make the most sense. We also decided, in our wise ways, that we would walk the bikes across the street to the entrance of Central Park, and not try and ride them on the roads outside the park. So off we set, walking these enormous tandem bikes across to the southwest entrance of the park. Once we were in the park, we quickly worked out a path to launch from. Stuart helped Gabriel onto his bike, and then helped me. The seat was up so high, I couldn't touch the ground with my feet. I got on, with Stuart's help, but then fell off again. Stuart had that raised eyebrow look of, "Are you serious? Do we have a problem here? You *can* ride a bike?" I tried to act calm, pretending it was all under control. Inside, I was starting to freak out. I asked Stuart if he could help me again. He held the bike while I stood on the gutter and climbed on. Stuart said he would jump onto his once Gabriel and I were right.

We started on a hill. I'm not sure why we did that. But we started on a hill, and so Gabriel and I were off at once. I was wobbling all over the path. I could hardly keep the bike upright. All of a sudden I remembered what it had been like for me trying to ride a bicycle in my childhood. I think my parents ended up giving my bicycle to the kid next door because I kept accidentally running over my brother! It had been twenty years since I had ridden a bicycle, and at this point, you could really tell. But it was too late now, so we were off. I didn't sense Stuart and Madeline behind us, but figured they would be there soon. I thought about stopping to make sure they were there, but then I worried about not being able to get back on my bike again and Stuart having to get off his, and thought he would get mad at me if I stopped. So I just kept riding.

Gabriel and I continued to ride and still Stuart and Madeline hadn't overtaken us. I asked Gabriel to look behind him to see if Stuart was there. The whole bike shook as he turned around. He told me yes, he could see Daddy. So I started to yell out to Stuart. I couldn't look around, because I was too unsteady on the bike to change my posture. I would simply yell out in front of me and hope Stuart could hear my voice. Every time we came to a turn or a corner, I would yell out and ask Stuart which way I should go. I couldn't hear his responses. I was literally flying by the seat of my pants. It was downhill and I was terrified. I kept asking Gabriel to see if Stuart was still right there. Yes, yes, yes, Gabriel would answer, "yes" every time I asked. We had been riding for almost thirty minutes and still I was flying ahead with Stuart behind me. Why wasn't he overtaking me? I didn't want to be in the lead here. I had no idea what I was doing.

I again asked Gabriel, in a very stern voice, if he could DEFINITELY see Daddy behind us. This time there was a pause. "No Mummy"... Oh dear. My heart raced. I went on to ask him if he had seen Daddy at all this whole time. Another pause. "No Mummy". My heart stopped! Sheer panic raced through my body. I got so upset that I lost control of the bike and steered straight into a lady who was running towards us on the other side of the road. Gabriel was flung off the back, I was on the ground, this enormous bike was on top of us, and this angry New Yorker was yelling at me. She didn't want to break her fitness routine, so she continued to run on the spot next to me, looking down and yelling. I was horrified. I tried to apologize but she didn't want any part of it. She ran off, disgusted. I picked up the bike, picked up Gabriel and walked to the side of the road. The path had now changed, and we were now faced with uphill sections. Great!

I had no idea where Stuart was. I had no phone on me, and no way of contacting him. I stood on the side of the path with Gabriel and the bike for another thirty minutes. I started to think I would try and walk the bike out of the park, return it to the hire place, and hopefully meet up with Stuart and Madeline there. I was just about to walk away, when I caught a glimpse of Stuart coming around the bend. My heart leapt in joy! That was until I got a better look at him. Stuart was riding towards us, with Madeline on the back, and he was covered in black grease, a look of thunder on his face. When they got to where we were standing, he yelled out, "Where did you go?" It was all too much. I had held it all in until this point but couldn't anymore. I burst into tears. Stuart tried to calm me down, while explaining that the chain on his bike had fallen off as he had gone to leave the path at the beginning. He had called out for me to stop, but Madeline had told him that she didn't think I could.

We got ourselves onto a patch of grass, and took a few moments to re-group. We were a long way from the entrance where we had entered the park, and we now had to get back there because the bikes needed to be returned to the hire place. Stuart helped me walk my bike to a level piece of path, and helped Gabriel on. I told him that I wanted him to go ahead of me this time. I could get on the bike myself. So as Stuart and Madeline took off, I jumped on my bike. Immediately I had the terrible wobbles again, and this time I crashed off the bike into a man running. Again, Gabriel and I were on the ground with the bike on top of us. Instead of being yelled at this time, the man was very concerned about us and helped us up. Stuart came back and we tried to get going again.

Once we finally got going, I started to feel a little steadier. We had made quite a spectacle though, and had roused the interest of quite a lot of people. As we passed people, ever so slowly, I could hear Gabriel on the back of the bike starting to pray. He was yelling out to God saying, "Dear Jesus, please help Mummy not to fall off this bike again." He kept repeating it over and over. I started to hear giggles and people genuinely found the whole thing quite funny. Meanwhile, Stuart and Madeline were so embarrassed, they had taken off up ahead, trying to not be linked with us.

It was well over an hour into this fiasco, and I was absolutely wiped out. I was not in any condition to be doing all of this riding. Gabriel was wearing a Liverpool Football shirt with the name Torres on the back. As I started to struggle to keep peddling, I heard people yelling out to us. "Come on Torres, you have to help your mum pedal." No wonder this bike was so hard to pedal, Gabriel was just sitting on the back doing nothing. I joined the people and yelled at Gabriel to help me pedal. He continued to pray, and did some pedaling in between.

Now there were a lot of people enthralled by what was going on. One lady yelled out and asked if my husband and daughter were up ahead on their tandem bike. So much for Stuart's plan to try and distance himself. The whole park knew we were together, and loved watching this whole thing play out. I would come to the intersections on the bike path where cyclists are supposed to stop for the pedestrians. I would start yelling out about fifty meters away that I couldn't stop and for people to watch out. It was crazy!

By the grace of God we finally made it back to our point of origin. There were cheers from the crowds as we finally got off and started to walk the bikes out of the park. We had come into this park as just another family joining the fun of the morning. We were leaving with hundreds of people in our wake, laughing and joking and talking about our family's antics!

God showed me very clearly that day, that no matter how big the platform, no matter how ferocious the crowd, no matter how hard it is to do what we have set out to do, when He is on us and with us we will stand out from the crowd. We will affect the lives of others, bringing a sense of joy to all those in our wake. It is when we stand out that God can use us to reveal Himself. If no one is looking at you, no one is seeing God in you. It's not about setting out to be noticed, it's being aware that God will make others notice you.

NO OTHER INGREDIENTS NECESSARY

Designer handbags don't need anything else attached to them. There isn't a need for bag tags or trinkets or anything else to try and add to the beauty. These items would only detract from the clean, stunning lines of the bag, rather than add anything to them. Prada doesn't sell accessories to make the handbag stand out. The beauty of the bag speaks for itself.

So too, you don't have to add anything to yourself to try and stand out and make yourself known. The world is always encouraging us to promote ourselves and put ourselves out there. Parents are pushing their children into the limelight. Everyone seems to be chasing his or her fifteen minutes of fame. The lengths some people go to in order to be noticed in this world can be frightening. It's not about what you can do to try and make a name for yourself; it's about making the name of Jesus famous. When you are less focused on the attention on yourself, and more focused on the attention of God, the sheer beauty of what He places on your arm to carry will bring a wonder all it's own.

Suddenly you will find yourself in places you never dreamed about, and standing in spaces that blow your mind. You will shake your head in amazement at a God who works in ways that are so different from ours. When the majesty and glory of God is upon you, and you are walking with the Prada of Heaven upon you, you will hold an influence, have a platform, be used in ways that you cannot attain any other way except by the hand of God. It doesn't matter who you know, how much money you have in the bank, what school you went to, who your family is, nothing will make you stand out more than the mark of God. If the designers at Prada need no help in creating a handbag that stands out in the crowd and lifts up the name of Prada, then how much more does God not need our help in creating a life that stands out from the crowd and lifts up the name of Jesus?

One of my favorite times of the year is March in Sydney, Australia. This is the time where thousands of women gather in the heart of the city and lean into God at Colour Conference, with Bobbie Houston and Hillsong Church. I have been attending Colour for a long time, and over the years have always had such an encounter with Jesus that each time it has left me different. On the surface, it would be easy to go to a conference like this one, sometimes with seventeen thousand other women, and feel completely lost. With thousands of other women all around, it would be hard in the natural to feel like you are a stand out, no matter what designer handbag you were carrying. But we serve a God who knows the numbers of hairs on our head. We serve a God who knows us no matter how large the crowd. And it is this God that looks not at the outward appearance, but at the heart. He doesn't see what the world sees as important. He sees what we carry on us from the shelves of Heaven.

At the conference this particular year, God spoke to me about my life in a profound way. It was the opening night, and Bobbie Houston was speaking to the conference and sharing a prophecy that had been given to her about the gathering of women before her. She said that one of the women gathered in Sydney, Australia in the Sisterhood movement was going to rise up and have the same anointing as Catherine Booth. It was like POW! In that exact moment I felt the Holy Spirit right there in my ear saying, "That's you…" My heart started to beat quicker as I looked around the room. There were seventeen thousand other women in the place, how could I think that Bobbie was talking about me? POW again. "That's you," the Holy Spirit whispered again.

I took that prophecy and claimed it as my own personal word from God. I have since learned the power of a prophecy and the idea that when a prophecy is spoken out from God, it is familiar to the angels. They recognize that it has come from God and it becomes their assignment to complete. There are some things that would not happen in this life if they were not spoken out in a prophecy first. I believe that God needed Bobbie Houston to speak out the prophecy that night, in such an enormous arena, for the angels that were gathered to make that prophecy their assignment.

Praise God for His anointing over my life, as He has taken me from Newcastle, Australia to stand next to Stuart as the ministers of a brand new outreach expression of The Salvation Army in New York City—a ministry that is fueled by the power of God and operates under the mantle and anointing of William and Catherine Booth.

It's not only when we have a hold on what God has for us that it's a stand out. It's a stand out whether it's on the shelves or over our arm. I know where I would prefer it to be! What about you?

THE RISK FACTOR

As with anything in life, with great privilege comes great responsibility. If you are going to stand out, there is risk attached. If you carry a Prada handbag, there is a greater risk involved in the day-to-day dealings of life. There will be a lot more concern for this handbag than there would be for a less expensive type. If an average handbag gets dirty, broken, or even stolen, there is definitely a sense of loss, but nothing compared to the feeling of having a Prada handbag dirtied, broken, or stolen. And so it is imperative that when you carry this bag, you are careful about where you leave it, what you allow it come in contact with, and where you go with it.

So too when we are carrying the Prada of Heaven, we need to be more mindful of what it is we are carrying and the risk factors associated with standing out in this way. We need to be careful to not leave that which we have received from Heaven laying idly around or resting on places that will leave it feeling dirty and marked. Don't go to that party, don't watch that movie, walk away from that conversation if it is going to affect and damage what God has placed on you. There is more risk involved when you have more of Heaven over you. You will become a greater target for the enemy to steal from you what you have. You need to guard and protect the promises and calling over your life, and understand the responsibility of what you carry.

I would not buy Madeline a Prada handbag, because she is not able to manage the risk and responsibility of owning such a treasure. God will not give you something you are not able to handle. The fact that you have been able to walk into the boutique and have the resource to purchase the handbag of your dreams, tells you that you have what it takes to carry this handbag well, and protect it, and guard it in Jesus name.

God showed me a vivid example of not just the privilege, but also the responsibility of standing out for Him. It wasn't until much later, after the event, that I understood just what God's message was to me.

Stuart and I were at the Bethel Leader's Advance Conference, and we were listening to Kris Vallotton preach. Everything he was speaking was such new revelation to us; we were literally devouring every word he spoke. As he preached, he shared a story about being known by coming under the authority of God. He used the passage from Acts 19:13-16, when a team of Jews were traveling from town to town casting out evil spirits and trying to use the name of the Lord Jesus. The demon actually spoke to them and said, "I know Jesus, and I know Paul, but who are you?" Kris was teaching that it is only when we come under the authority of God that we have an identity in the supernatural. The demons did not know him.

It was from this passage Kris taught we should be known in hell and famous in Heaven. That if we come under the authority of God, the demons will know us, and we will be famous with the angels. He shared a personal story from several years ago where a homeless man in a phone booth said loud enough for Kris to hear, "Kris and Cathy Vallotton are here." The demons knew who he was.

It was in that moment, sitting in that meeting at Bethel that God spoke to me and said, "I have already shown you this." Instantly God brought into my mind a day I had never been able to truly understand. After our first Skype call with the leadership of The Salvation Army in New York City, Stuart and I were invited to come to New York and meet the leaders face to face and have some more formal interviews.

Everything seemed to be happening so fast at this point, and before we knew it, we were on a plane to New York City to meet with the leadership about the calling God had laid on our hearts. The day of the main interview, Stuart and I had been up early and were praying and covering ourselves, and placing ourselves completely into the hands of God to outwork His perfect plan.

We were staying in a Salvation Army facility, which was an old people's home on the Upper West Side. As we came out of our room, we entered the elevator all dressed ready to head down to 14th Street. The trips could take quite some time in these elevators, because there were a lot of elderly people getting in and out at every floor. As the doors opened yet again, an elderly lady stepped into the elevator. She took one look at me and her whole face contorted into an angry, fierce pose. She glared at me and started to make growling noises. She then turned and put her head right into the corner of the elevator, and started rocking back and forth on her heels. Every couple of seconds she would turn around and snarl at me, making disturbing noises and faces. Stuart and I were so tense, he positioned himself closer to me, later admitting that he thought he might have to step in front of me to protect me from her attack. It never came to that. She stood and watched me walk out of the elevator on the ground floor, seemingly not being able to move herself.

We arrived at 14th Street early, and decided to go and stand in front of the golden gates where we had stood just six months before, trying desperately to get inside. Now in just six months, we were not only going inside, we were going to the boardroom on the executive floor, to speak with the leadership of The Greater New York Division about stepping into this space in ministry. How amazing is God!

As we stood there, talking and praying together, a man came up to us. He said hello and introduced himself as Oz. It was then that he looked at me with a huge grin, and put his head into his hands saying, "Oh, it's you. I can't believe it's you. I love you." We just stood there unsure of what was happening. Then he looked up, still grinning, and started to speak to us, mainly Stuart. He told Stuart there are so many people on these streets that need someone like Stuart to come alongside them and help them do life well, that people like him needed a mentor like Stuart. He said there are many people in America who send money overseas to help starving children, and that's great, but there are people on these very streets who need help.

Stuart looked at him and told him we were just about to go into a meeting so we would be able to do that very thing. Oz thanked Stuart, he smiled a huge smile at me again, and off he walked.

As I sat at Bethel and remembered that day again, I saw these occurrences with a fresh understanding. I was known in hell and famous in Heaven. Whatever was on that lady in the elevator, knew me. And it was angry! Oz was an angel, sent from God to give us a message, but when he saw me, I was famous to him!

That is the ultimate stand out right there. You walk with such an anointing and inheritance and treasure and resource of Heaven over your life, that it changes everything. You look different to everyone that you encounter, you point people to Jesus, and you are known in hell and famous in Heaven.

THE INNER LINING

Not every Prada handbag looks the same, but every Prada handbag has the same lining. There is a signature Prada material used to line the inside of all Prada handbags. They all may appear to have differences on the outside, but inside they are covered in the same thing. We may all carry different things. What you carry will look different from what I have chosen off the shelves of Heaven. But at the heart of it, it is all the same. The designs may differ, but the inner workings are the same for everyone. I love that God custom designs just for us. He asks us to dream with Him, tell Him what we want, and He gives us the desires of our heart. At the very core of it all, no matter what our dreams look like or what shape His inheritance takes, we all have the same portion of His presence and His love.

On Pentecost, the believers sat in the Upper Room waiting and praying for the arrival of the Holy Spirit. When The Holy Spirit did arrive, every person in that place received the exact same portion of the Spirit upon him or her. Each one had a tongue of fire above their head, each one heard the sound of a rushing wind. And when they burst out of that room, (because you cannot be contained in a room when the power of the Holy Spirit is upon you), they each started to speak in foreign languages as they were individually led by the Spirit. They all spoke different languages, but were lead by the same Spirit. We will each carry different aspects of the inheritance of Heaven, but it will come from the same God, driven by the same Holy Spirit and will make the same name of Jesus famous.

7

THIS SEASON'S MUST HAVES

"He has given me a new song to sing, a hymn of praise to our God. Many will see what he has done and be amazed. They will put their trust in the Lord." Psalm 40:3 (NLT)

The fashion world is broken up into two main seasons. Spring/Summer and Fall/Winter. At the start of each season, New York and Paris host an event called Fashion Week that brings all of the top designers together and showcases what will be coming out in an upcoming season. In New York, Fashion Week is held in Lincoln Center, and it is all very exciting and glamorous. There is a buzz in the city around this time of year, and if you walk past Lincoln Center you will see lots of red carpet, photographers, tall women, celebrities, and lots of great fashion. It's one of the hottest tickets in town!

The whole premise of Fashion Week is the understanding that

fashions change from season to season. Designers come up with new themes and concepts and styles, and men and women all around the world follow the trends that are featured on those runways. No matter how successful and wonderful last seasons fashions proved to be, designers embrace the new day and work hard to bring a new layer of design to the fashion table. Top designers never just sit back and rest in the knowledge they had a great line last season. They push forward, building on the momentum from the past and taking it further than they ever have before. They introduce new looks and styles, and their name and credibility is built stronger with every new season they produce.

There are some pieces that transcend all seasons and all designers and are staples in every fashion landscape. The crisp white button up shirt, a little black dress, a pair of denim jeans, a beautiful pair of tailored black pants, a shiny pair of black stilettos, these are pieces that fit into any season, in any line, of any designer. They are signature fashion pieces and they will indeed stand the test of time.

The same is true for designer handbags. With every season come a new range, a new color palette, a new look and feel. There is a different feel for Spring/Summer than there is for Fall/Winter. The mood of the handbags reflects the feelings of the season. Again, there will always be the classic designs and patterns that fit into any designer handbag range, but the designers will continue to work to produce fresh vision and lines that are exciting and new.

NEW STOCK HAS ARRIVED

God is constantly giving us new, fresh, vision and anointing and inheritance with each new season of our lives. It isn't enough to gather all of the resource we have managed to accumulate, make a big Prada purchase, and then live off that purchase for the rest of our lives. Don't get me wrong, you can do it. Sadly many people do this very thing. They give everything they are for a time, and are filled and equipped and resourced, ready to walk in and take what God has shown them on the shelves of Heaven. But as soon as they receive this amazing gift from God's hands, they go into maintenance mode. There is a relief and relaxation knowing they made it, they've got something of value, and they hold onto it for the rest of their lives. They never think to stretch themselves for more.

I see people all the time living life from a platform of what was done in the past. And while it is a great thing to treasure all the goodness and blessings you have taken hold of in the past, that Prada should be part of your classic, staple, signature collections, which are added to by the new things that are coming out of the design house. Jesus came that we may have life, life in all its fullness. A full life knows no limits to what can be taken hold of and added to the armory of our inheritance.

We limit God in our lives because we think we should be satisfied with what we already have. Yes, we must be grateful for what we have every moment of every day, but God is the God of "morning by morning new mercies I see." He is the God who asks us "to bring a new song to the Lord." Each new day represents a new opportunity to take hold of something more. But if you aren't in the boutique of God, you won't know or see what else is available. It is when we are in that intimate space with Him we see the vision of more. God says that without vision, the people will perish. When something perishes, it starts to rot over a slow period of time. It gets old, smelly, and leaky, disintegrating into a pile of disgustingness. Without having a vision of what God has for you in this season, you will start to become old, sour, smelly, and will disintegrate into a person no one wants to be around. You don't have to be old to be perishing. You can be in your 20's, and yet be stinking to high heaven!

NEVER GIVE UP YOUR SEAT AT THE RUNWAY

Fashion Week gathers everyone into one place, and sets the vision of the season. What I would give for a ticket to Fashion Week. Many of my friends feel the same way, trying desperately to get into one of these shows. If you were offered a couple of free tickets to attend a Fashion Week show in New York, would you take them? My guess is you probably would. Imagine if we were that desperate to get into a space with God, into His house, to see the new vision He is setting before us.

It is when we see the new things God has for us that we will go to new levels to take hold of what is there. We will release our lives and situations to God, we will walk through whatever narrow door He has for us to enter, and we will stand in the midst of the greatest boutique available on earth—the church which is a reflection of Heaven. There, we will be so filled with vision we will take hold of what we want, knowing we have got the resource to cover it and then some!

God will not look at you and wonder why you are back for more. He will delight that you are taking hold of everything that He has created for you to live the life He has called you to. This past Christmas was our first Christmas spent in New York, and I have to admit I went a little crazy with my kids. I just love buying gifts for people, and my kids are my favorite people in the whole world to buy for. I loved going to the store and picking out things I just knew they would love. I loved creating little bundles of really fun things, and imagining how they are going to use them, where they would put them, and all the amazing times that would come from these gifts. As I wrapped their gifts, I imagined the looks on their faces when they opened them, and it got me so excited.

I have phenomenal kids. They've built up such a level of resource that they are able to come to days like Christmas morning and take whatever they want without worrying about the cost. They are our constant sources of encouragement and love. Never once have they complained or wined about leaving all of their family, their friends, their church, their school, their home, selling their toys and bikes and furniture and clothes, and moving to the other side of the world into a land where everything is new, and life is far from comfortable. To sit with my little boy with two empty suitcases and watch him decide what he would take from his bedroom that was filled with so much is something that I will never forget. Our kids love us, they love God and their faith and trust completely blows my mind.

Let me paint a fictional scenario. Imagine if we all sat down on Christmas morning, near the tree, with the twinkle lights on, the carols playing and the camera ready. Madeline and Gabriel opened their first present from Stuart and I. There was so much excitement, just as I had envisioned. There were squeals of delight and laughter, joy and excitement at the gift they had just received. The wrapping paper was cleared away, the gift laid next to them. It was time for the next present. I had strategically ordered the gifts and was saving the best until last. But instead of taking the next gift, they decided that they didn't want to appear greedy or wanting more or ungrateful for what they already had, so they left the rest of the presents under the tree. Imagine if they left that space near the tree, and didn't come back into that area again. The gifts would just lay there, unopened, unused, unloved. If only Madeline and Gabriel knew what was under the tree for them! If only they knew they were eligible for so much more.

There are so many delights in Heaven that God wants you to have. He has them ready and waiting and wrapped and strategically ordered for your life, and He wants you to come and take hold of them. But too often, we take hold of the first one or two, and think we are done. You are not done! You are not finished! There is more to your story. There is more to your inheritance. There is more to what is available for your life. Keep raising the resource, keep stepping into the boutique, keep reaching for more.

TIMING AND SEASONS

There are different styles of handbag for different stages and occasions of a woman's life. In some seasons, we need a nice compact handbag that will fit perfectly over our arm to hold the essentials of a day's outings. Other times we will need a nice small clutch to fit in the palm of our hands and add a touch of glamour to an evening dress. Then there are the seasons of being a new mum, with all of the paraphernalia that goes with having a small child. These are the seasons you need to have the biggest handbag you can find. I'm talking bags that could very easily double as airport carry on luggage. Then there are the seasons when your arms are filled with papers, folders, and documents and you need a handbag you can fling over your shoulder and leave your arms free. Ultimately, you will chose a handbag based on the season of life you are in.

Likewise, there are different promises and purposes and inheritances that God has for you in different seasons of your life. God knows what you are going through, and He knows the perfect promises that will add to the platforms of life He has called you to live.

No one wants a handbag that is completely impractical and useless for your situation. No matter if it is Prada, Louis Vuitton or Chanel, a clutch just isn't going to cut it for a mum heading out with a one year old. It just isn't. No matter how spectacular it may look, no matter how many other women have one, it just isn't the right bag for that person, for that time, for that place.

That is why we cannot sneak over the sheepfold and try and take the promises and inheritances of God. We need to come into an intimate space with Him, holding the resource we have achieved, and then see what it is He has for us to take hold of. God's plans are perfect, His ways are perfect, and His heart for you is perfect. He will lead you right to where you need to be. God didn't bring us to New York until we were ready to take hold of all that was there for us to receive.

New York had never been in the boutique before for me. When I would come into a space with God and take things from the shelves He displayed before me, there was never the option of New York. He was reserving that particular Prada for when I was able to carry it well. I wasn't in the right season of my life before that point.

I was taking hold of my Pradas, but they were different styles and designs. I was taking hold of the promises and inheritances and callings of a blessed and holy marriage, I was taking hold of my precious daughter and then my son, I was taking hold of a beautiful home filled with love and laughter, I was taking hold of gifts in preaching and leading, I was taking hold of gifts of friendship and holidays and all sorts of other things that God had for me. That's what I was taking hold of when I came to Him and gave Him my everything and dared to ask for more.

That is why it was so important to keep up to date with the new things God was creating and that He was setting vision out for. If I would have settled with what I already had taken from the shelves, I never would have moved into a space where I saw the Prada of New York City.

Maybe you are still carrying an enormous handbag when God is encouraging you to take hold of a clutch. Don't miss what God has for this season of your life because you are holding too tightly to what He put over your arm in the past. Make room for more. Jesus didn't feed the four thousand people, and have just enough. He fed the four thousand and then had twelve baskets of overflow. God is a God of the overflow. He is a God that has more up His sleeve than you can ever hope to imagine or know. As long as we keep releasing everything to Him, and following Him, and going wherever He leads, we will see new promises and opportunities before us with every new day and season of our lives. And it's all there for a reason. Whatever He allows you to see on the shelves is the perfect accompaniment to your life, and will be threaded perfectly throughout your days. Rest in Him and know that He knows what is best for you.

GOD'S SURPRISES!

Remember how fun it used to be to get a surprise? Maybe you still get surprises, but mostly as we get older, the opportunities for receiving surprises diminish. God still loves surprises. He loves to be able to show you something you never expected to see. Glimpses through the windows of Heaven will reveal new things, and once we step into the place where He is, we will be continually surprised at all there is, and the new things God has in store for us. You will feel like a kid in a candy store when you truly come into the place where God calls you to stand and to look and see and taste how good He is, and how good what He has on offer for your life is.

From that New Year's Eve night where so much of our journey started, I have been keeping a journal and writing all of the promises that God has spoken over our lives. Day after day, as I would step into that intimate space with God, I would take hold of new promises and declarations over my life. It wasn't a window shopping experience, making lists of the things I would love to have one day, it was an ultimate shopping experience, where I completely took a hold of these promises, made them my own, and didn't have to worry about the cost. I took them into my world, my space, and made them a part of the way that I did life. I was getting the most amazing collection of designer handbags, never for once thinking that I could exhaust God's supply. There were new seasons being unveiled all the time with so much vision that I could hardly wait to get into the word and pray and worship and give every day!

One of the precious Prada's God gave Stuart during this time was the promise of Deuteronomy 6:10-12. It reads, "So it shall be, when the Lord your God brings you into the land of which He swore to your fathers, to Abraham, Isaac, and Jacob, to give you large and beautiful cities which you did not build, houses full of all good things, which you did not fill, hewn-out wells which you did not dig, vineyards and olive trees which you did not plant—when you have eaten and are full—then beware, lest you forget the Lord who brought you out of the land of Egypt, from the house of bondage."

A SIGNATURE PROMISE

At the time of taking this promise and inheritance, Stuart and I were both filled with excitement and wonder at all God had given us in these few verses. This was one of those passages we would always have. Others would come and be added to this, but this was one of those times when we stood in awe of God, and were genuinely excited about the days to come. This was a high-end designer handbag if ever I saw one.

We shared these verses with others, and told about the promises God had given to us in the design of these words. We believed it and lived it and felt excited about all that was to come from it. It was early in our journey and we held onto these words not yet understanding the full picture they painted.

It wasn't until we had been in New York for nearly seven months that Stuart and I were sitting one night, and sharing our hearts with one another. Stuart had just finalized the sale of our Australian business, and we were coming into a season where there was literally no safety net. God would have to be our provider like He promised He would be, or else we were really in big trouble. The sale of the business was great, but it meant the end to the income we had been receiving.

There are times when Stuart and I sit together and the waves that are all around us distract our attention from the face of Jesus. We are totally out of the boat. Every step we walk in life is a step that we can't possibly do in our strength, in fact it is impossible for us to do. It is only by looking into the face of Jesus and having the faith to believe that where God calls us, He will enable us to walk. We have been walking on water for the past seven months, since the first day we arrived in New York City. And while it has been the scariest time in my life, it has also been the most exciting, exhilarating, rewarding, and blessed time. It really is living life to the full.

It always works that when either Stuart or I is struggling with doubt and fear, the other is standing strong, ready to recite the promises of God, testify to what God has already done, and love and encourage the other through the hard times. We were sitting on the lounge together and were in one of those kinds of spaces. We opened the Bible, and started to read the promises that God had given us in Deuteronomy. As we read the Bible that night, as we examined the Prada more closely, we saw another aspect we had never seen before.

LOOK CLOSELY

God started to point out the truths of what had already been accomplished, what we could already see, and then the things we are yet to see. When we studied the passage, Stuart reminded me that we had to look at the order in which God was laying out these promises. The first promise listed was, "The Lord God would bring you into the land that was promised to your ancestors." Yes, God had brought us into the Promised Land of New York City. He had brought us into this place where The Salvation Army first landed in the United States of America. It was in Battery Park that the first representatives from The Salvation Army in England landed on American soil. Yes, we were on the land God had promised to us.

Next, the passage says He would bring us into this land, "to give you large and beautiful cities that you did not build." God has given us space, authority, and position within New York City. It is the biggest and most beautiful city I know, and He has brought us to the land of America, to give us the city of New York to outwork the dreams and callings and destiny He has placed over our lives. We didn't build this city, we have had nothing to do with the foundations of The Salvation Army in this city, and yet He has given us the platform to take this city for Jesus, working through The Salvation Army.

The passage then goes on to promise, "houses full of all good things, that you did not fill." If you have ever tried to find an apartment in New York City, you will understand how hard this process can be. It is not for the faint hearted. I'd put it right up there with trying to get your child into a good high school in Manhattan. When making arrangements with The Salvation Army about our transition into New York, it was agreed that we would be provided with temporary housing for the first six months. By then, we would have had time to get on the ground and find ourselves our own place to stay, and be in a position to organize rent expenses, etc. Only a couple of weeks before we left Australia, we found out the accommodation that had been organized for us was in a suburban part of Queens. We were in shock! We just assumed we would have temporary housing in Manhattan, as we had no car and no idea really of navigating any of the other Boroughs.

We explained that a place in Queens was not going to be suitable, but we were informed there was nothing else available at the time. So we requested a room at the old people's facility on the Upper West side, and moved into a one-bedroom unit with our eight suitcases and four pieces of hand luggage. We were so appreciative of having somewhere to stay, but realized that for the children's sake, we couldn't stay here very long. So we instantly set off, with three different agents, trying to find the perfect rental apartment. Some life-long friends were in New York at the time, and they joined in our efforts and helped us race all over the city. We had a couple of days before school started for the kids, and we were trying to organize school supplies, bank accounts, cell phones, and everything else you need to survive, and we had to find an apartment on top of it all.

We were out everyday, for hours on end, looking through apartment after apartment. We just couldn't find anything we thought would be suitable. We walked up countless flights of stairs, we looked into third bedrooms the size of closets, we felt nervous in the hallways of huge buildings, we tried to work out where the nearest subways were, we smelled horrible smells, we felt squashed into living rooms, and we nearly collapsed when we saw the monthly rent prices. We knew we would have to compromise on what we thought was possible, but it was getting disheartening. In our minds we had this picture of a loft style apartment with separate three bedrooms situated close to where we could walk and subway anywhere we wanted to go. It seemed a million miles away.

That is, it felt impossible until we received a call from an agent who told us there was something we could look at. It had a walk-up of three flights of steps, and the agent wondered if that was a deal-breaker for us. We said we would still look and didn't want to rule anything out at this stage. We were running a little late, and as we ran up to the block, we recognized this part of the city. This was one of our favorite spots in Manhattan; we knew this area really well. We walked up the stairs and walked into an *amazing* apartment. It was so much better than anything we had seen so far. It had three bedrooms downstairs with an ensuite off the main, and when we walked upstairs, there was one big open area, in a loft kind of style. There was the added bonus of a private rooftop area. We instantly knew this was a place we could make our home.

It was crazy expensive for us, but reasonable for Manhattan, which is what we had to go off at this stage. We wanted to initiate the paperwork as soon as we could, so we started to fill out forms and understand what would be required from us. It was at this point when our hearts sank the most. Because we had been planning on having six months of housing provided for us, we left Australia not worrying that our home had not been sold. Now that we needed to get into a rental, we needed to have a lot of money ready up front as part of the initial set-up costs on a lease. We quickly realized that we would not be able to provide the money that was required to secure this property. Our spirits were heavy. We prayed and asked God if this was the home He had destined for us to live in, then He would make a miracle happen so that we could be able to take up this lease.

Stuart asked to speak to the landlord personally, and explain our financial situation to him. We were able to afford this place, we just had capital tied up and were unable to pay the security money required. The landlord asked for a reference from us. We really didn't know anyone who could vouch for us in the city at this point, so we forwarded a letter written by the Territorial leader of The Salvation Army in Australia, which spoke about us and our characters. To say it was a long shot is really understating it. What would a business man care about a letter from a church leader in Australia, telling him we were people of high spiritual and moral character? There was no mention of whether we could afford to pay our bills, or any talk of money at all. We prayed over the letter, and believed that it would do whatever it was God needed it to achieve.

By a miracle, the landlord accepted our terms and drastically reduced the financial commitment he needed from us at the time of signing the lease. We had found a home in New York City, and it was fabulous. When going through all of our finances in order to secure the lease, we quickly realized that we had no money to buy furniture. In fact, we had very limited funds to buy anything at all. We would be able to get the bare essentials like sheets, towels, plates and glasses, but other than that, we were going to have to get comfy sitting around on the floor until our home in Australia was sold.

God had other ideas. As we were in the process of finalizing the lease requirements and signing contracts and papers, the landlord offered to leave all of the furniture in the apartment of our use. We could hardly believe it! There were lounges, rugs, a huge dining room suite, display cabinets, even cushions! It was all amazing furniture of such a beautiful quality, and it was all there ready for us to move straight into. All we needed to buy was mattresses for our beds. A fully furnished apartment in the heart of Manhattan, a place where our friends walk into now and say, "Oh wow! This place is amazing!"

It was beyond our wildest expectations.

We look at the promise that was given to us many years ago and read the words, "houses full of good things, that you did not fill." Yes and Amen! That's what I am talking about. That was the next level of Prada over our lives. Yes, you could just be happy to have been brought into this land. Yes, you could be satisfied to then just stop and take on the city that He has given you. God you have led us to so much. Thank you God for this. And then go about and try and make the best you can, fending for yourself. Or you can expect God for more, show up fully resourced in His boutique and take the next level. God is saying, "come back there's more!" Yes, there's more. There's an apartment waiting for you that is filled with good things you did not fill.

The building is small. There is a restaurant on the ground floor, our landlord is on the next floor, his sister-in-law is the next floor, and then us. It's like our own little NYC family. We feel completely safe, and have the chance to be friends with the owner of our apartment. We could not be happier.

BUT WAIT, THERE'S MORE

The next part of the promise talks about "hewn out wells that we did not dig." This is where we are now. There is a promise that there will be wells where we will find water to keep us alive. The thing about wells is that you can't see the amount of water that is in them. You simply lower the bucket and draw up the water. You don't see the rivers or dams or lakes of water, you see only the tools to draw the water to yourself. This promise is particularly profound for us at this point. We don't see the resource sitting in all sorts of bank accounts out before us. We don't see lakes of finances, sitting there waiting for us to draw on. Instead we see a point or an avenue in which money can be drawn for ourselves to survive. There is a level of faith at work when you lower a bucket down a well and expect there to be water at the bottom. And every day we must exercise our faith and believe that whenever we draw down into the well-spring of what God has for us, there will be resource there for our needs.

My spirit starts to leap as I read the next part of the promise, the next Prada to hit the shelves for us to take hold of. This promise states, "vineyards and olive trees that you did not plant." We have gone beyond the land, and the city, and the house, and the water to survive; now we are going to a whole other level to the vineyard and the olive tree. Praise God for Prada that looks like vineyards and olive trees. This is the above and beyond stuff right here. This is the promise of a Prada that stands out like no other. This is the promise of blessings beyond what we can even imagine.

The vineyard is the place where wine is made. The first miracle Jesus ever performed was to turn water into wine, to turn the ordinary into the extraordinary. To turn the survival into the thriving. To turn the routine into the celebration. Jesus was at a wedding when this took place. The framework and platform for his very first miracle was a wedding: A celebration of a new union, a celebration of love, a celebration of a brand new chapter in the lives of the bride and groom, a separation of the bride and groom from their respective families, and the start of a new family. This was the start of a covenant relationship between them and God, a celebration of a union that God has joined together. Water was not suitable for this occasion. This occasion called for wine. God is giving us the promise of wine. He will provide the wine for our lives, the blessings of celebration to mark the beginning of this celebration of love, covenant relationship with Him, and the new chapter He has created in our lives.

When we first heard the call in New York City about coming to fill the Temple once again, God used the Parable of the Wedding Feast. He was framing this calling over our lives to build His church in terms of a wedding, a place where water is turned to wine, a place where miracles happen for the very first time. This is our platform. This brings a level of excitement that I find hard to contain.

God continually spoke to us about not putting new wine into old wineskins—the wineskins would burst and the new wine would be wasted. We can't come into this arena and try and build His church using the same frameworks and guidelines as before. We can't try and fill the old wineskins with the new wine that we see Him produce through miracles. Both will be ruined. We are called here to do a new thing—to build His church in a new way, to house miracles that have never been done before.

The vineyard in the Bible is often related to the church. When the ten spies set off to explore the Promised Land, they came back with differing views. Eight of the spies came back citing stories of the giants they had seen and all the reasons why it was never going to work out for them to go in and try and take the land. The last two spies returned carrying a huge stick between their shoulders with giant grapes hanging from it. They were adamant they were well able to conquer the land.

When Stuart and I came and surveyed the land, like spies entering the Promised Land, we could have easily seen the giants and the obstacles and impossibilities in the situation. Many people tried to caution us about what we were getting into. But instead we chose to have the victor's mindset that said, "We are more than capable of taking this land." Out of two million people, two men ever entered the Promised Land. Two men carried giant grapes back. Two men held onto the promises of God.

God is promising a vineyard we did not plant, a vineyard producing a wine that must not be put into old wineskins. Is this a daunting task? Yes! Does this make us feel nervous and fearful to go in and stand against the giants in this land? Yes! But God has promised us grapes so big it will take both of our strength to carry them. When voices of opposition have come against us, our response has always been: "judge us by our fruit." If we dreamed up this vision on our own, then it will come to nothing. But if it is truly of God, there will be no stopping it. God has promised a church that produces fruit that is so much bigger than anything we have ever seen, a church that defies the normal and the natural, a church that will be filled with blessings and miracles that no man can carry alone. Grapes produce wine, so when God gives us giant grapes, He gives us what we need to produce a lot of new wine!

We read a story in the Gospels about fisherman who had been fishing all night in their own strength and had not caught a fish. They were cleaning their nets when Jesus told them to go back out and drop their nets on the other side of the boat. They went back out under the direction and authority of Jesus, and their nets became so full, they could not carry all of the fish they had caught. Other boats had to come and help them with the load. Jesus is promising us a haul so big, with miracles so profound, we will not be able to carry the weight by ourselves.

A ten-year-old girl prophesied over Stuart and I at Bethel. She said when she looked at us, she saw the image of trapeze artists. There was so much faith and trust that we needed to put into one another. She told us God had put us together because of how well we work together, and others love to watch us because when we work together it makes a beautiful picture.

Stuart and I have been married for eighteen years, and we have never experienced the attacks we have had on our marriage since moving to New York City. We have been bombarded with attempts from the enemy to break us apart in so many crazy ways. But God is stronger than any attempts made against us, and He has kept us bound in His love and protection. I understand why our marriage is such a threat to the devil. We can't do this alone. God needs Stuart and I to work together, to carry this fruit together, to storm the promise land, to take hold of the blessings, to use the new wineskins, and to be brave and courageous together. And when we follow Him, and trust Him and trust each other, people will stand back in awe.

Trapeze artists don't have a safety net. Part of their magnificence is the risk that something could go wrong. But they know nothing will go wrong because they have complete trust and faith in the bond they share. You can only ever have that level of trust when God is the author and the protector of your bond. Without God in the equation, you have two failed people. When God is in the middle, everything is different. So many women ask me what the secret is to a marriage that thrives and shines so beautifully after eighteen years. That is the secret right there. God is in the middle, therefore Stuart and I can trust our marriage with our lives and use it to carry all He has for us, and all He has for the church of The Salvation Army NYC.

God used a wedding feast to call us into giving our lives to His plans for The Salvation Army in New York City. He framed the call to fill His house with the picture of a wedding. Right from the outset, God was promising a place that was in full celebration mode, celebrating love and miracles and abundance and blessings and excellence and a marriage that would be used to invite the people to come.

Oh how my soul praises God and the extravagance that is available to those who are willing to give their lives to it.

The second part of that promise is not only vineyards that we didn't plant, but also olive trees that we didn't plant. The olive tree is seen to be one of the most valuable trees. God is promising there will be such value in our lives and ministry and the work He is doing. There is a richness, brilliance, prominence, fruitfulness, shine, and anointing that comes from an olive tree.

It is from olives that are shaken and pressed, that oil comes—the oil of anointing. As the final layer on this mind-blowing promise, God is promising a level of anointing over us and within His church. And this level of anointing will resound with the nation we live in, as the seal of the United States of America features an olive branch. We claim this promise and see the oil of anointing poured out in ways we have never seen before, for such a time and season as this.

8

TAKE IT OUT OF THE DISPLAY CASE AND LET'S GET STARTED

"Jesus came and told the disciples, "I have been given all authority in heaven and on earth. Therefore, go and make disciples of all the nations, baptizing them in the name of the Father and the Son and the Holy Spirit. Teach these new disciples to obey all the commands I have given you. And be sure of this: I am with you always, even to the end of the age.""" Matthew 28:18-20 (NLT)

A designer handbag is a beautiful thing. To look at a Prada is to truly see beauty personified in a handbag. The design, shape, materials, zips, buckles, straps, lining, badging—everything about this bag is positively gorgeous. I have never been inside a Prada boutique and seen an ugly bag. There is just an essence of beauty in every handbag that comes out of that design house.

An integral aspect in the beauty of such a handbag is the layers and dimension it carries. This is not just a pretty handbag, with no real depth or strength behind it. This is a fully functioning, well-equipped, strong, reliable, resilient tool to aide in the rigors of a woman's day-to-day life. As petite and pretty and delicate as some of these bags may seem on the outside, the truth is they are built to be reliable and dependable and able to cope with any situation you may take them into.

We must never forget this. We must never treat these handbags like superficial, limited objects. This would be missing out on so much of the real beauty these handbags are made to show. A Prada handbag is made more beautiful when the strength of its character and design is shown.

This is so true of not only designer handbags, but also the women who carry them. You have been hand crafted by a God who loves you and designs beautiful things. Nothing that ever comes out of His design house is ugly. And the most amazing part of the beauty God gives to each and every one of us is the depth and layers that it holds. It is so much more than a superficial prettiness. To be pretty is one thing, to have a real beauty is quite another.

Beauty isn't dependent on any other factors. It doesn't need fancy adornments or additions or attachments, it stands alone. It is the very essence of what something or someone is. If you are a person of beauty, you have beauty threaded into the very core of who you are. You aren't scared about losing it or having it fade, diminish, or be tarnished because of tough work.

THE VINTAGE FACTOR

In fact, real beauty comes into it's own the older it is, and the strength it displays no matter what environments it is in. The only thing more expensive than a brand new designer handbag is a vintage designer handbag. Designer handbags that are many years old, and still in good condition, are worth an absolute fortune. There is an incredible value attached to vintage beauty. One of our friends works for the Ralph Lauren vintage store RRL in Greenwich Village, and we are astounded at the stories he tells us of the value attached to vintage designer clothing.

The world wants to tell you that beauty is limited to an outward appearance, and once that has faded, the beauty fades as well. This is a lie that has women all over the world trying desperately to hold on to something that is not a real reflection of true beauty. True beauty never fades, in fact it becomes more beautiful the older and deeper and richer and braver and more courageous and bold it becomes. A vintage handbag has established it's identity, and its value comes from the depth and continued beauty in that identity. When we get older as women, there is such an incredible value within us from the depth and beauty in our identity.

Part of the way our identity is strengthened and cemented is the different environments and challenges we have faced over the years. We can't ever be scared of going into tough places or circumstances for fear of diminishing our beauty. It is in these very times when our beauty is developed and enhanced and magnified. There is nothing we can ever buy, or attain, or adorn ourselves with, that will ever match the beauty of a life well lived. A life used to the full. A life worthy of the calling God has placed upon our lives.

God designed you, while you were still in your mother's womb, to live the life He set out for you to live. So the brightest and deepest your beauty will ever be is when you are living and experiencing and fulfilling all God destined for you. You are at your optimum when you are living the optimum version of your God-orchestrated life.

Some people keep getting more beautiful with age. As the days and years go by, their beauty becomes more intensified and brilliant. This displays a life that is experiencing more and more of what God had designed and created that person to be. The person who is living a God life is developing their God beauty, and it is more magnificent than anything a surgeon's knife can create. It's real, it's authentic, it's a stand out.

Other people radiate a beauty in their younger years, but this beauty never deepens or grows or develops. These are lives that have settled or strayed or not tapped into the fullness of the life that was set out before them, and the beauty has not had a chance to grow and ferment and develop.

Knowing the mighty inner strength that is at the core of a Prada handbag, we will not be afraid to take it with us on the paths that are laid out before us.

NOT JUST A PRETTY FACE

What God has for us, the Prada available for our lives, is not just surface attractive. There is a beauty, depth, resilience, strength and, magnitude at the very heart of everything we take hold of from the shelves of Heaven. We must never fall into the trap of thinking that what we have taken a hold of, with the resource we have given God, needs to be treated with white gloves. We do not need to worry about making a mark on it or damaging it in some way. If you are delicately holding what you have from God, trying to tip-toe through life with it, you have no idea what you are actually holding.

You are not in the possession of a display item. You are not the owner of a fragile promise that could break at any time if put under too much pressure. Cheap things break. Expensive things last the test of time. You don't want to pay much for something you don't expect to last long. If you pay a lot of money for something, you expect the value to be good. What you hold in your hand from God you have paid a high price for. Don't ever forget that. When you paid that price, you guaranteed you had something of real value.

In fact the moment you step into the boutique with God, you can't go wrong. No matter what the dream in your heart looks like, no matter how the desires within you hope for it to look, the quality is always going to be of the highest possible standard. Jesus said himself, "In this world you will have trouble, but take heart for I am have overcome the world." Yes, these dreams and promises and inheritances are going to come under some attack. Yes, they are going to cop a bruising from time to time. Yes, they are going to have some pretty big blows. But take heart, Jesus has guaranteed they will pass the test every single time. Jesus has guaranteed no matter what gets thrown at it, it will not break. Jesus has overcome. Jesus has already won the fight. Any battle ever raged against you or the dreams, promises, destinies, or inheritances over your life is a losing battle. You have the victory in Jesus.

We are more than conquerors through Christ that strengthens us. Greater is he who lives in me, than he who is in the world. I could recite scripture after scripture that guarantee this Prada is not ever going to break, my sweetheart. You want to see the fine print of all of this? You want to know if there is a catch? The fine print is this. The fine print tells you that what you have is one hundred percent guaranteed with the full backing of the hosts of Heaven. What you have purchased will never be destroyed. What you have purchased is a true treasure.

Therefore don't store your treasure up in the things of this world, where moths and rust can eat and destroy, instead store up your treasure in Heaven, where moths and rust cannot touch it. This is the ultimate guarantee. This is the assurance that what you have invested in cannot be touched by anything in this world. It is safe and protected and guarded by God and the angel armies. I have never been more aware of angels than I have since we arrived in New York City. His angels are everywhere, and they are ferociously guarding all we have over our lives and over our church.

REMEMBER WHAT'S HANGING OFF YOUR ARM

It is imperative we don't ever forget what we have. You must never forget what you have a hold of. Don't be like Dorothy who walked through so much, never knowing the full extent of what those shoes could do. We have something extraordinary in our hands; it is literally out of this world. It was not created in this world, it will not fall victim to this world, but it has the power to change this world. Use it to it's full potential and you will see a beauty emerge that is more magnificent than you can ever imagine.

Watch your marriage flourish, watch your children sparkle, watch your career shine. Watch your ministry take off, watch your friendships blossom, watch every single thing you have picked up and taken hold of operate in the supernatural.

IT'S SHOW TIME

This is not the time in history to place all of our Prada's in a display case and never actually use them. They are not collector's items, they have a purpose. I have always found it to be odd when people have things but never use them. It's like owning a four-wheel drive but never taking it off the road, like having toys that are never taken out of the packages. I knew a family once that had a living room set up with beautiful furniture, but they never went in there. You and I were born at this point of history for a reason. We are the people who will usher a revival of the church into the world. We cannot afford to have these treasures and not use them. We can't afford to have display cases filled, but destines empty.

It's so much bigger than us. This isn't just about you missing out on all God has for you. It's the impact on your world if you don't use what you have. In Matthew 8, we read about the disciples in a boat one day with Jesus, and they were going across the lake to the other side. Jesus was tired, and grabbed a pillow and fell asleep. As he was sleeping, a huge storm came over the top of them. The disciples were terrified, and woke Jesus up, yelling and carrying on, asking him if he cared whether they died or not. Jesus rebuked the wind and the waves, and the storm was gone in an instant. He asked the disciples why were they so afraid, did they not have faith?

This story in Matthew is entitled "Jesus Calms the Storm." The story that appears in Matthew 8 directly before this one is entitled "Jesus Teaches about the Cost of Following Him." The disciples had paid the cost to be followers of Jesus. They had put down their lives, so as to have the life Jesus could offer. They had released their lives fully over to God, and in exchange had picked up the greatest treasures, promises, inheritances, and declarations of Heaven. They had the Prada of Heaven right with them, literally in the same boat! And yet when the storm raged, they went into full panic mode. The disciples were rattled, letting the storm terrify them, until they woke Jesus up and stood in the miracle He then performed.

Why did the disciples get into such a state of panic? Jesus was with them; he was on the very same boat. They were not only holding the Prada of Heaven, they were with the darling of Heaven himself. And yet the storm reduced them to fearful, yelling, faithless, accusation-throwing men. How could this happen? Jesus wanted to know where their faith was.

Again, this test was not about Jesus needing to see how the disciples would behave under pressure, he already knew. It was about revealing to the disciples themselves how they were carrying what they had. Jesus had just established with the disciples what it had cost them to follow him. They all boarded that boat knowing they had paid the price, had already come up with the resource to take hold of some pretty spectacular stuff. They knew what they had.

Jesus wanted to show them what they were doing with what they had. This story reveals that the disciples had their Prada's in a display case. They all had a Prada, that's for sure, but it wasn't being used to help them navigate the paths of their everyday lives. Jesus was on the boat with them, he was asleep on the boat. But when the storm raged, their initial reaction was panic. They had Jesus, but they acted like they didn't.

What is your immediate reaction when storms hit? Do you go straight to the feet of Jesus, or do you get there eventually? Do you run straight to him, or do you run around flapping your arms in panic for a while and then remember to go to his side? There is no need for us to waste our time, energy, emotion, or livelihood on falling victim to panic in the face of the enemy. The enemy's strategy is always for you to discount what you have. If the disciples could so easily discount Jesus when he was literally sleeping right under their nose, how much easier is it for us to discount what we have? Sadly, there are some who never seem to be able to break through the panic barrier. They spend their entire lives in a state of nervous anxiety and never fully understand the peace that could be theirs. All the while they are running around with the full measure and portion of Heaven right there, but they never, ever engage it.

The storm only stopped once the disciples had woken Jesus. It is one thing to have Jesus on your boat, it is another thing to engage with him. It is one thing to own a Prada, it is another thing to use it. No matter how amazing what you have is, no matter how great the cost you paid to receive it, if you aren't going to use it, it is worthless to you in your times of greatest need. The disciples may as well have had a statue of Jesus in the boat that day if all they were going to do was run around and panic. It was only in their engagement of him that they were able to experience his power. If you aren't ever going to use a Prada handbag, you may as well have a beautiful picture of one framed on your bedroom wall. Same thing. So many people have pictures of Jesus hanging in their homes, they wear crosses around their necks—they have all sorts of representations of Jesus. But what good is any of that stuff if you don't engage with the real thing? It is only Jesus himself that will change your life and your present circumstances. It is only Jesus himself that will calm your storms. The disciples had him and yet didn't use him. Don't have his promises and inheritances and yet not use them.

At the very start of the chapter at Matthew 8, the heading is "Jesus performs many miracles." The disciples were sitting in a boat in the middle of a chapter of miracles. They had seen Jesus perform miracle after miracle, and yet they still hesitated to engage and use him. We can sit in the midst of a life filled with miracles, and yet still hesitate to use and engage him and what we have through him.

BE THE ONE

If only one of the disciples that day had approached Jesus earlier, it would have affected everyone else on the boat. It would have only taken one disciple to wake Jesus up sooner, and the rest would have had their panic and trauma reduced. It only takes one person to use their designer handbag. It takes one person to take hold of the promises and blessings and provisions over their life, and it will change the environment for everyone else in their world.

The moment the storm was cleared that day, the moment the seas were calm again, the relief was felt not only by everyone on the disciples' boat, but every other boat on the lake. Other boats had followed Jesus and the disciples out onto the lake that day. They would have been experiencing the storm as well. It was up to the disciples to engage with Jesus so that calmness could be released over the entire lake, for everybody else there.

As leaders in our families, workplaces, schools, colleges, churches, friends, we have to make sure we have our boat in order so that when the storms come, a peace can wash over our world as quickly as possible, and others can lean in. When you have a Prada, you are equipped to be able to change the atmosphere in your world.

When you have the promises of Heaven, the provision and inheritance and destiny and goodness, you have the power to make a difference in the world around you.

When we are a church that carries Prada, we have the ability to use what is in our hand to calm the waters for everyone who follows our boat with Jesus on board. When people see Jesus with you, when they know you have Jesus in you, they will follow you. Don't lead them into storms that go on with no end in sight. Don't lead them into a place where you change from a person who is calm and together, into a raving, panicked, insecure, spiteful crazy one.

THERE ARE ENOUGH BOATS; WE'LL ALL GET OFF

You have the privilege of holding a Prada; you also have a responsibility to use it. The people on board the Titanic didn't use the rowboats to their full potential, and as a result, many lives were lost. If you don't use what you have been given, lives could be lost. What you have in your hand is bigger than you can ever imagine. It is so much bigger than just you. If you take that Prada of songwriting and yet never share your songs with the world, there will be people who needed to sing that didn't. Whatever your Prada looks like, whatever design it may be, it was given to you for purposes beyond you. You are just the blessed one that gets to carry it. It's not about you, it's not because of you, it's God working through you. Once that reality becomes your framework, you will never leave what you have resting idly around, sleeping in your display cases.

There is a powerful image that William Booth would use to explain the world around us. It was the picture of a tumultuous sea, and a whirlpool dragging people down. There were many, many people drowning. In the middle of this chaos, there stood an island where people could find safety. Some of the people who were on the dry land were reaching into the sea to try and rescue those that were dying. But sadly, there were many on dry land that had turned their back on the ones perishing in the waves, preferring to be comfortable and safe. Where are you in this picture? What are you doing with what you have received? Are you using it to make a comfortable life for yourself, or are you using it to reach the ones still in the sea? The people on board the rowboats from the Titanic could hear the screams of others as they drowned in the freezing sea, but they never went back. They stayed dry and comfortable and safe. I can't imagine how they lived out the rest of their days. I can't imagine how the sound of those screams could have ever truly left them.

The world is screaming out for love. The world is screaming out for joy, the world is screaming out for hope, peace, kindness, care, provision. The world is screaming out for salvation. The world is screaming out for the Prada of Heaven. You have it. What are you going to do with it? Will it become part of your personal collection, to have and to hold, to keep you warm and safe and comfortable? Or will it be the very lifeline you use to save the perishing and the lost?

God calls us to co-labor with Him, to fight the good fight, to run the race, to gain the prize. The part we play is not greater than the war we are in, but it is so much bigger than ourselves. What God requires of us is to get our hands dirty. Our part isn't to just walk around carrying the Prada, having fun with the luxury of the greatness. Our part is to use the Prada on the streets, in our homes, in our churches, in our workplaces, in our schools, in every place that our feet tread.

When King David was a small boy, he faced a giant called Goliath. Goliath was a storm in so many people's lives. Goliath was causing fear and anxiety and heartache and disruption in the lives of others. And one small boy took his Prada and used it to partner with God to change the atmosphere and the people's lives. Before David went out to battle Goliath, King Saul tried to give him his armor to use. But after David tried it on, he refused to use it, instead picking up his slingshot and three stones.

CUSTOM FIT

The promises, purposes, and inheritances over my life are custom fit for me, I can't just simply hand them over to you. What you have received, from the boutique of Heaven, is for you; you can't give that to me. We can look at other people and want so desperately what they have, but when it comes down to it, what they have isn't for you. David tried on the armor, tried to walk in it, and quickly realized he wasn't going to be able to do what he needed to do in that framework. All it takes is for us to try and operate even for a few steps within someone else's calling to realize we are not going to be able to get anywhere in that framework. We will not only be risking our own future, but the atmosphere of so many others.

My Nanna used to be really funny about anyone else trying on your wedding rings. She would be adamant that you should never allow someone else to put your rings on. Your wedding ring is your personal symbol of the union that you share with your husband or wife. No one else can simply wear your ring, and then hope to have a marriage like yours. This ring symbolizes what you have. Another ring will form the identity of someone else's marriage. You cannot simply take hold of the same verses of scripture or calling or prophetic word that has been given to someone else, and expect to have what they have. When we first told people we were moving to New York, and explained the calling over our lives, there were many, many people who said they wanted to come too. But after taking a few steps in that calling, they realized that it wasn't for them. They would not be able to do what they needed to do, wrapped in that calling.

So little King David went out to face Goliath with what he had been given by God to carry, a sling shot custom fit for him. And with this slingshot he stood face-to-face with the enemy. The slingshot was in his hand, and he was ready to use it. He didn't have a picture of it, he didn't have the idea of it, he didn't have notebooks describing what it would look like, he didn't have daydreams about it, he didn't have it safely tucked away at home for fear of it getting broken if this turned out wrong. He took his slingshot into the front line of battle with him. That is why he had it. That was the whole purpose of him ever having it. All of those times he had played with his slingshot and hunted bears with it and hit targets and whatever else a young boy does with a slingshot, all led to this one moment. What a disaster if he didn't take it with him!

We need to take our Prada, our top shelf, next level, above and beyond gift from Heaven, and use it on the front line of battle. We have it for such a time as this. Everything we have ever used it for has been preparing us for the day we would step up to the battlefield, ready to face the enemy. Don't be afraid to use it. You have this. You know what to do with it. It's yours, it was created for you, and it is exactly what God needs you to use to win this battle.

I came to New York carrying my Prada. It was mine, God created it for me, I knew it well. Although when coming into this space and standing face-to-face with this city and everything that was working against us, there was a massive temptation to doubt what I had was going to be enough. There was a temptation to take on the Prada of those ahead of me and older than me, feeling that I would be better equipped if I had what they had used. But God challenged me and told me that if David could kill a giant with a slingshot, then I could pull down any enemy with the calling and anointing and promises that I have lived carrying. I had to fight with what I had, which was exactly what was needed in the battlefields I stepped onto day after day.

When the time came, and David was out on the battlefield, we read part of what he spoke out to Goliath in 1 Samuel 17:45-46. It reads, "David shouted in reply, "You come to me with sword, spear, and javelin, but I come to you in the name of the Lord Almighty—the God of the armies of Israel, whom you have defied. Today the Lord will conquer you, and I will kill you."

This was David's battle cry, and this is my battle cry, and it is your battle cry. When we are faced with an enemy so big we can't see around him, we stand with our Prada on our arms and this battle cry on our lips.

THE POWER OF A LABEL

David identified what Goliath was coming at him with. He

identified and named the tools Goliath had in his hands. When we are faced with the enemy, we need to stand and identify and name the strategies and lies and schemes that he is using against us. Instead of just standing in the presence of the enemy and losing ourselves in fear, we need to ask God to give us wisdom and discernment to see exactly what it is we are fighting. Just like David saw and discerned that Saul's armor was not right for him in this battle, David saw each piece that Goliath was using in his attack. We need to see every element, every person, every strategy the enemy is using in his attack on us.

It was when David identified what the enemy had that he realized he had something not only that Goliath had rejected, but was stronger. David identified himself as coming under the authority of God. He positioned himself in this way, and thus established his identity in hell and fame in Heaven. He came under the authority of God, so he would be able to act on His behalf. And David established that Goliath had defied and rejected this authority. It says in the scriptures that Jesus was the stone the builders rejected. Now David would pick up a stone and use it to conquer the enemy before him.

First, identify what it is the enemy is using against you. Then you are able to establish that what you have and what authority you come under is not only the very thing the enemy rejected, it's stronger than anything he has. You establish your identity as a child of the King, as a servant of the Most High, as a representative of God. As you declare your position under God's authority you establish your identity in hell and fame in Heaven. Then you take up the stone—the power of Jesus and the Prada God has for you, the very thing that the builders rejected—and use it to conquer the enemy.

David declared that God would conquer Goliath, and he would kill him. This is David co-laboring with God. This is David getting his hands dirty, doing what he can do and must do, but leaving God to do what only He can. God is the conqueror. God has conquered the power of sin and death over lives forever. He sent His one and only son Jesus to die on the cross so that whosoever will, may be saved. The conquering is done. We must let God be God in our lives and conqueror the enemy before us. But that is only half of the victory.

If the first half of the victory is God conquering Goliath, the second half is David killing Goliath. God conquers, David kills. David fires the stone, which lodges in Goliath's forehead and causes him to stumble and fall face down on the ground. God has promised He will level the mountains before you. He doesn't say He will remove them, but He does say He will level them. God leveled Goliath before David. He took the giant man and laid him flat on the ground before David. He took a figure so tall David couldn't see anything else around him, and placed him at David's feet so he was able to see the way clear.

MOUNTAIN MOVER

God doesn't remove the mountain, but Jesus told us we could. In Matthew 21, Jesus tells us that if we have faith the size of a mustard seed, we can say for a mountain to be lifted up and thrown into the sea and it would happen. We need faith to kill our Goliaths. We need faith to remove our problems and our enemy.

As soon as Goliath had lost his stronghold and his footing and his position in front of David, David had the faith to run in, grab Goliath's sword and kill him by cutting off his head. He had a window of time before Goliath could have risen again, and taken the same position in David's outlook and landscape and life.

As soon as God levels mountains in front of us, we need to have the faith that runs in and flings them into the sea. When the enemy that looms in front of us is brought crashing down by God, we need to not hesitate and wait and wonder if we can do it. We can't be caught up in if we should go now or if this is really how it works. Don't linger, thinking about if our kids will be alright, is there will be enough money in the bank, if anyone is going to like my work, if anyone will come, if we will find friends, if I will disappoint people. He who hesitates gives room for the enemy to rise up again! This is a vicious pattern. The enemy looms, intimidates, causes destruction in your life, God conquers, the enemy is brought down, you hesitate, the enemy rises again, the enemy looms, intimidates, causes destruction in your life, God conquerors, the enemy is brought down, repeat repeat repeat. Stop this crazy cycle! Have the faith that runs into the battle knowing that God has gone before you. He has conquered and given you the victory to have and to claim.

David killed Goliath by grabbing Goliath's own sword and cutting his head off with it. God says He will work all things together for good, for those who know and trust in Him. The very thing the enemy comes against you carrying, is the very thing God will give you access to in order to kill the enemy's plans in your life. What the enemy plans for evil, God will work for good. Goliath planned to kill David with his sword. God had different ideas. God conquered Goliath and leveled him flat and useless so that David's faith could propel him to take hold of the sword that was destined to kill him, and kill the enemy instead. Those who live by the sword will die by the sword. The enemy wants to plan attacks against you. He will be defeated by those very same plans.

When God takes the power and the presence of the enemy and levels it before you, run in and kill. Don't watch those shows, don't go to those places, don't go through that drive-thru, don't go on those websites, don't engage in those conversations—kill the things God has conquered in your life. When God conquerors, it doesn't mean it has disappeared, it means its power has been leveled before you. You may still want to give in to the destruction, but have the faith to run headfirst into the problem, and cut it off once and for all.

THE FINAL BATTLE CRY

And so, my precious one, you have everything you need to live a life of victory, abundance, and overflow, walking in His promises and purposes and callings daily and living with the inheritance of Heaven over your life.

Walk into the boutique, pick out your Prada, hang it on your arm, speak out the battle cry and take the world by storm. You've got this.

Forever may you say, "Make mine Prada!"

ARE YOU FEELING LIKE YOU'RE ALL DRESSED UP WITH NO PLACE TO GO?

If you have just finished this book, and there is something stirring within you wanting to take some Prada and get out there, I want to get you started on your way.

Maybe you have never had any type of relationship with God. You may never have acknowledged or looked to Jesus in your life. So much of what you have just read is so new to you, revelation that you have never known. I want you to know that in a moment, everything can change. In a moment you can come into a real and authentic relationship with Jesus Christ and as you give your life to him, he will show you the way to discover and take hold of your Prada. There is a prayer we need to pray together.

Maybe you made a commitment to God a long time ago, but it has diminished as the years have gone by. Once there was a love and fervor for Jesus, but now there are only distant memories or even bitter hurts. It takes but a moment to bring the ruins of your relationship with God back to life. The time you have spent apart will be forgotten in an instant by a God who loves you more than you will ever know. It's time to come home, beautiful one. There is a prayer we need to pray together.

Maybe you do love Jesus with all your heart. Your life is all about honoring God and bringing Him glory. But you are carrying no Prada. Instead of having the very best of Heaven hanging off your arm, you are carrying the ordinary and mundane. It's time to shake off the dust from the land where you have settled, and step into the above and beyond. There is Prada waiting for you. It's for you, but it's for purposes bigger than you. Your world needs the Prada that you will carry. Let's go shopping! There is a prayer we need to pray together.

LET'S PRAY TOGETHER

Dear Lord,

I come before you now and lift up my heart to you. Thank you for loving me and dying on the cross for me. Please forgive me for the things I have done wrong, as I receive your love and mercy over me. I want to be a Christian, a follower of you. I want to follow you all the days of my life. I lay down my life before you now, and ask you to come upon my life in ways I have never known or experienced before. I pray that you would show me and teach me and lead me, to the purpose and destiny you designed for me before the world was even formed. Please make up any time we have lost together and draw me to your side for now and forever. Jesus, please show me the way to not only take hold of all that is mine in Heaven, but give me the faith and courage to take it to the streets and change this world for you.

Amen.

If you have just prayed this prayer, please send me an email and let me know. I would love the honor and privilege of celebrating with you and cheering you on as you step into the greatness of our God. Please contact me at: jody@makemineprada.com

Made in the USA
Middletown, DE
14 September 2015